Linda Applewhite's
Architectural INTERIORS

Linda Applewhite's
Architectural INTERIORS

Transforming Your Home with Decorative Structural Elements

LINDA APPLEWHITE

Gibbs Smith, Publisher
TO ENRICH AND INSPIRE HUMANKIND

Salt Lake City | Charleston | Santa Fe | Santa Barbara

To my life partner, soul mate, and best friend, Marshall,
who believes in me and all my crazy ideas . . .
and to Biff, Tina, and my pal Joey.

First Edition
11 10 09 08 07   5 4 3 2 1

Text © 2007 Linda Applewhite
Photographs © 2007 Claudio Santini, unless otherwise noted

Published by
Gibbs Smith, Publisher
P.O. Box 667
Layton, Utah 84041

Orders: 1.800.835.4993
www.gibbs-smith.com

Designed by Dawn DeVries Sokol
Printed and bound in China

Library of Congress Cataloging-in-Publication Data
Applewhite, Linda.
   Linda Applewhite's architectural interiors : transforming your home with
decorative structural elements / Linda Applewhite 1st ed.
       p. cm.
   ISBN-13: 978-1-58685-885-8
   ISBN-10: 1-58685-885-8
   1. Architecture—Details. 2. Interior architecture. 3. Architecture,
Domestic. I. Title. II. Title: Architectural interiors.

NA2840.A65 2007
728—dc22

2006038776

Contents

Acknowledgments

THIS, MY FIRST BOOK, has been a long time coming and was possible only with the support, commitment, dedication, and friendship of an amazing group of people. I thank Jackie Schaeffer for her outstanding wordsmithing and phenomenal computer skills; Pat Emrich for her fabulous artist's eye and incredible photo sleuthing; Angela Luchini for her awesome disposition, resourcefulness, and ever-steady holding down the fort; Caroline Pincus for her calm, centered wisdom and outstanding skill; Patricia Gilda for helping set me on my path; Naomi Epel, who guided and encouraged me from the beginning; and Marlene Caldes for her spirited insight; Laurie Soldmann, who was always there to listen; Juli Fields for hearing my voice and truly seeing who I am; and Stuart Piontek, who has never stopped supporting and believing in me.

These acknowledgments would not be complete without including architects Fran Halperin and Eric Christ, who taught me so much; artist John Hull, who made many of the exceptional cabinets on these pages; Shawn Man Roland, truly a fine artist who can transform an unattractive glulam into the most fabulous 100-year-old beam; Arno Cornillion, for his exceptional decorative painting skill; and Tom Maddox, for his resources and "before" photos.

In addition, I want to acknowledge a truly exceptional artist in his own right, Mike Stone, whose amazing innovation with tile and stone graces the pages of this book and who I have had the honor of working with as my friend and partner in so many creative endeavors.

I would also like to acknowledge the countless architects, contractors, tile setters, drywallers, plumbers, electricians, carpenters, cabinetmakers, and painters I've learned from along the way.

I owe much of this book to my clients, who have trusted me with their homes, challenged me to grow, and inspired me to work with them side by side to create their visions.

And of course many thanks go to my editor at Gibbs Smith, Jennifer Grillone, for her commitment, support, guidance, and never-ending patience; Suzanne Taylor for her innovative vision; Madge Baird for taking my call in the first place; Katie Newbold for her amazing sense of spirit and cooperation; and the entire staff of Gibbs Smith, Publisher, who worked so diligently on this book.

And finally, I'd like to thank all the photographers for their wonderful images, especially Russell Abraham for his amazing magic, and Claudio Santini, whose special way with light fills the pages of this book . . . *bella, bella, bella! Grazie,* Claudio!

INTRODUCTION

From Characterless 1950s Tract House to European Country Cottage

I HAD ALWAYS DREAMED of buying an old, unloved house with lots of character and turning it into a beautiful, treasured home. My husband, Marshall, and I had been living in the San Francisco Bay Area for eight years and still hadn't come close to making that dream come true, due to the high real estate prices. Then my mom suddenly died and left us just enough money to make a down payment on a small and what I hoped would be unique property with "good bones."

And so our search began. I couldn't wait for the open houses every week so we could peek inside old homes and check out their "bones."

(RIGHT) BEFORE: Hidden deep in a forested canyon, completely covered with trees on a street named Clorinda, a special old house materialized.

(ABOVE) AFTER: Clorinda emerged in full view with a strong presence when we cut back the foliage and painted her bold ocher, green, and white.

(RIGHT) BEFORE: Clorinda's original living room had 8-foot ceilings, a contemporary opening cut in the wall, and an unassuming white brick fireplace that commanded little presence in the room.

(FACING PAGE) AFTER: The newly remodeled living room boasts pitched ceilings with 1-inch x 12-inch shiplapped pine and 3-inch x 6-inch recycled beams. Bookcases were added on either side of the fireplace, and an antique mantel gives the focal point new presence. Walls were textured to look like old plaster.

By "bones" I mean architectural details such as beams, arches, niches, pitched ceilings, interesting windows and doors, beautiful moldings, distinctive fireplaces, columns, or cabinetry. "Bones" are architectural character that is incorporated into the structure of a home and that distinguishes it from all others.

But my dream of finding a home with good bones began to fade as we saw one older home after another that had been remodeled and the original architectural character altered. These homes had lost their special patina of age and had become shiny, new, and soulless. We grew discouraged.

We decided to broaden our scope and reluctantly started to consider a new home. As we journeyed through dozens of new houses, we found that many looked alike—each one a series of boxes grouped on a foundation, with eight-foot ceilings, tiny moldings, and carpeted floors. They were usually devoid of architectural detail, and if they did have any, it often seemed false and pretentious. In time I simply gave up. I just couldn't find a house that felt right, that came close to my vision. But when you let go, something magical often happens, something appears. In this case, I recognized it immediately. Hidden deep in a forested canyon, completely covered with trees on a street named Clorinda, the special old house materialized.

Well, it wasn't exactly as old as I'd envisioned, and it didn't quite have the character I had imagined. It was in fact a 1950s tract house with eight-foot ceilings, practically nonexistent moldings, and a small, nondescript white brick fireplace. It had linoleum floors in the kitchen, white Formica countertops, dark 70s-era cabinets, and an ironing board that dropped from the wall. But here was the real clincher: a previous owner had attempted to make this simple cottage into a contemporary model home. All the openings between rooms had been raised to within a few inches of the ceiling and drywalled without moldings, which gave a schizophrenic, modern feeling to the fifty-year-old cottage. Installed in the dining room was a pair of large doors with a heavy black frame, solid smoked glass, and brass handles. Above the doors, which opened to the garden, was a 10 x 6 rectangular brass light fixture with a black metal frame and twelve Plexiglas disks that hung like periscopes six inches below the fixture. An elaborate panel on the wall afforded the option of lighting the disks in the shape of an

(RIGHT) BEFORE: Clorinda's dining room before the remodel, with the contemporary smoked glass doors and the exposed framing left by the enormous high-tech fixture that had been removed.

(BELOW) AFTER: The remodeled dining room with a pitched ceiling and fat arched wall leading into the newly added family room. Recycled French doors with complementary side lights replaced the contemporary doors, while a light fixture custom made to emulate an old French meat and poultry hook makes a bold statement above the dining room table.

X, a square, or a rectangle. Wow, I thought—disco dining! The real estate agent excitedly shared that the fixture had come from a hotel ballroom in San Francisco. Little did she know, we were already planning how we would replace it.

The other new window in the house was a frosted metal slider in the exterior bathroom wall. The tub shower was a very deep, tiled rectangle with no slope for relaxing. Fortunately, the bedroom had not been touched, but, unfortunately, two windows sat side by side behind the only place a bed could go in the room.

Still, it was love at first sight. Despite the fact that it looked just like all the other houses in the neighborhood, and what little character it did have was distorted by trying to make it into something it was not, my heart sang.

Regardless of the low ceilings and thinly framed walls, the small amount of light that came into the house, and the lack of connection to the garden, my gut confirmed what my eyes couldn't yet see. It had really good bones and, yes, this was home.

(ABOVE) BEFORE: The dark '70s-era cabinets contrasted with the white Formica countertops, linoleum floors, and refrigerator.

(LEFT) AFTER: The new kitchen boasts glazed and distressed knotty pine cabinets with rust-finished Bouvet hardware. The ceilings were faced with 1-inch x 12-inch shiplapped pine, and two skylights provide light from above. Antique French paver tiles cover the counters, and an old peely-paint green door found at a salvage yard keeps the washer and dryer hidden from view.

(LEFT) BEFORE: The old master bedroom had two large double-hung windows on the only wall that could accommodate a bed.

(FACING PAGE) AFTER: Clorinda's master bedroom is transformed with a raised ceiling, textured apricot walls, intriguing architectural elements, and a chandelier. The original windows were split apart and reinstalled on either side of the bed.

The first thing we did when we moved into the house we came to refer to as Clorinda was take out the huge, high-tech light fixture in the dining room. I simply couldn't live with it. This left a large, gaping hole in the ceiling, which I did live with for two and a half years. Each night and weekend, we'd talk endlessly about what we wanted to do to our new house, followed by what we could afford to do. We kept affirming enthusiastically to each other and to our friends as they visited that, despite all appearances, the house really did have good bones and lots of potential. Though some friends looked skeptical, we continued, undaunted.

Clorinda Transformed

The majority of the remodel itself ended up taking six months. After much discussion, planning, and saving money for almost three years, we finally began construction, during which time we lived in our tiny basement, without a bathroom or kitchen! It was a huge undertaking, chock-full of creative challenges and gut-wrenching decisions. We were blessed to work with an amazing architect, Fran Halperin, who somehow managed to reconfigure a few existing rooms, adding a master bathroom, a third bedroom, and a family room, while expanding the footprint of the house by only 300 square feet. Meanwhile, I completely redesigned the interior. I had never remodeled a home before and was overwhelmed by the process, yet I found that I loved every moment of it. In the end, through a remarkable team effort, Clorinda had morphed from a characterless 1950s tract house into a European country cottage.

We had exposed her bones, making good use of her multiple peaks and hidden angles by pitching ceilings in the living room, dining room, master bedroom, and new family room. We had added beams and lintels, a fat wall and arch, and a niche in the kitchen. We had opened her up to the garden with wonderful old windows and doors and brought in light with six new skylights. We had embellished her with substantial moldings and installed interesting cabinetry and bookcases throughout. We had covered her plain brick fireplace with an antique mantel and installed an old recycled column where a wall once stood.

(RIGHT) BEFORE: The only bath room had a metal sliding window with frosted glass and a deep rectangular tub with no slope for reclining.

(FAR RIGHT) AFTER: The remodeled bathroom sports a skylight above the bathtub that reflects light off the handmade high-gloss apricot and rust colored tiles, cheering the small room with sunlight. The curved iron element holding the decorative fabric panel was custom made by a local artist. It hides a second bar that supports the actual shower curtain, which pulls across on a wire that connects to the matching iron hook on the right, providing no interference to the incoming light.

It was the resulting remodel of Clorinda that prompted me to write this book. Although I have since assisted dozens of clients with remodels and the design of new homes, Clorinda was my first remodel and led to a career of helping people see, uncover, and create good bones whether they are building, remodeling, or just looking to embellish or enhance their existing architecture.

And by the way, that unassuming 1950s tract home that looked like all the other houses on the block, was totally lacking in architectural interest, and had a high-tech twist put on its unsuspecting fifty-year-old cottage bones has now bared its bones so many times that I have lost count: on HGTV, in *Sunset Magazine, California Home and Design, Better Homes and Gardens, Creative Home, The Best of Sunset Outdoor Living,* and even on the cover of *House and Garden Thailand.* Design books that have featured Clorinda include *French Country at Home, Lowe's Idea Book, Sunset's Garden Book,* and *Better Homes and Gardens—The Design Book,* which is touted to be the number one selling design book in the country. So, it just goes to show that you should *never* underestimate the potential of an unassuming, lackluster, high-tech '50s tract house with good bones. It might just be the house of *your* dreams.

Surprisingly, Clorinda was mine. Most importantly, through the process of working on Clorinda and other homes, I learned that it is essential to respect architecture and not try to make a house something it's not. It's important to look above, below, and beyond the surface of a structure. The homes I've had the privilege of working on have taught me how to bring beauty and uniqueness out of a variety of architectural styles. I've learned that many homes have good bones and are just waiting for their beauty to shine. Others have not-so-good bones, but they can shine, too, with some creativity and vision.

The chapters that follow look at the various areas within a room where bones can be revealed, enhanced, or actually created. You'll notice that the rooms pictured in this book range from modest to grand—from lofts to cottages to estates—and from contemporary to rustic to whimsically eclectic. But no matter what the style or price range, they all demonstrate how critical the bones are and how they can be worked with and embellished to best advantage. In some, we added interesting windows and doors, which made a clearer connection to the land. In others, we installed beams and lintels or columns and pilasters to give the structure a feeling of strength. In a few, we enhanced the fireplace to become a stronger focal point, created unusual cabinetry to give structure to a room, or added moldings and railings to add more interest. In the text, I explain how to work with your home's existing bones and where to consider adding new ones. I also explain some of the basic issues involved in home construction and design so that you'll know the right questions to ask as well as the materials and methods that will and won't work in your home.

Whether you are looking for a home to transform, building a new home, or remodeling your current home, this book is meant to inspire and guide you. There is also food for thought for those who just want to create more elegance with bigger, more elaborate moldings or put in a set of French doors to connect to the garden. You say you don't have a big budget? Adding architectural interest can be as simple and inexpensive as buying a can of paint and using your imagination.

(ABOVE) BEFORE: An exterior view of the smoked glass doors with their heavy metal frames. A contemporary overhang had been installed above the doors, conflicting with the existing lines of the cottage.

(LEFT) AFTER: The rear view of Clorinda with the new family room added to the left and a pair of old French doors and sidelights replacing the former contemporary unit in the dining room to the right. Architect Fran Halperin, of Halperin & Christ, San Anselmo, California, replaced the modern overhang with a pitched roof.

OPENINGS *of All Kinds*

"May your walls know joy; May every room hold laughter and every window open to great possibility."

—MARYANNE RADMACHER-HERSHEY

FACING PAGE: A true divided light window frames the opening of the small dining room in this remodeled 1920s Mediterranean home, adding character without diminishing the view. The massive window and distant view of the hillside amplifies this diminutive yet elegant gathering area.

AT THE TIME I REMODELED CLORINDA, I had owned my design business for four years but had worked primarily with the furnishing of interiors and not with the actual structure of homes. The remodel of Clorinda introduced me to the creative opportunities that open to you when you can actually change a home's structure and, yes, the power in that as well—true interior design. The ability to pitch ceilings, knock down walls, and create new openings for windows and doors was thrilling and had so much more impact than picking ball fringe for pillows. I was hooked.

In my first professional construction project, I learned that as soon as a building plan is completed and approved, one of the first decisions to make is what type of windows and doors to install. This is because of the long lead time required to manufacture them. A home's openings are among its most significant architectural details and dictate the tone and feeling of a structure. Windows and doors not only determine the amount of light and air that come into a home, they also establish connection to the site and surrounding area. One of my favorite design mantras has always been "It's not just the way a home looks, it's the way it feels." Little affects a structure's presence and feel like the quality and style of its openings.

Stylish Openings

So, how does one go about choosing windows and doors? I don't believe in rules, but I do believe in principles. One of the most important principles I live by when working with homes is to *always respect architecture*. Never try to make a structure something it's not or incorporate elements that don't reflect its original architectural character. The style of the windows, doors, and even skylights should echo the style of the house.

You can have a beautifully built home, for example, but if you install inexpensive windows and doors, the structure will feel cheaply built. Whatever you do, please try to avoid low-quality windows—the ones with thin or flimsy frames or sashes. These are often made out of lightweight aluminum or plastic and may have snap-on plastic grids to simulate a true-divided-light window. They will always bring down the look of a house. Similarly, if a home's windows and doors are dated, the home will feel dated. For example, unless they are classic in design, windows and glass doors that are stained, leaded, frosted, or opaque can become dated over time. Avoid this, if at all possible. If you install windows that don't harmonize with the architecture of the home, like a metal sliding glass door in an old Victorian, it will always look wrong. Select window and door styles that complement your home's architecture.

COMMON WINDOW STYLES

Casement—Hinged at the side and opens outward along its entire length.

French—A hinged pair of sashes that extend to the floor and open in the middle.

Single Hung/Double Hung—One or both sashes slide vertically past the other. In a single hung window, only one sash moves while the other is stationary.

Sidelight—A fixed panel window, usually next to an operable door, such as a front door.

Single Slider/Double Slider (also called Gliders)—One or both sashes slide horizontally past the other. Good for areas where a swinging sash or frame would interfere with access or furniture placement.

Transom—A stationary fixed panel that is typically placed over a door to allow light to pass through.

True Divided Light—A window style in which multiple individual panes of glass are connected with horizontal and vertical bars (or muntins) to comprise a single sash.

Contemporary Blomberg casement doors open to a patio with a mountain view. The transition is seamless and allows the bed to be rolled out on the patio for sleeping on starry nights. Transom windows over the doorway and adjacent vertical windows expand the opening and view. A deep green door-frame color was selected to blend with the mountain.

French doors opening out to the pool double as windows placed behind a pair of chairs in a family room where seating space is limited. These doors provide good bones and a solid backdrop for furniture placement, yet enhance ventilation and connection to the outdoors.

For example, if you have an old Mediterranean home, French-casement doors with true divided light glass panes would be an appropriate selection. Contemporary yet substantial metal sliders would complement a modern home, and double hung windows would be appropriate in a Craftsman-style bungalow.

The style you choose for your windows and doors deserves considerable time, research, and deliberation. Remember, good design repeats itself. If you are remodeling and your home has some original windows or doors that are attractive and complement your home's architecture, simply order windows that match them. Don't be talked into a more modern and cheaper style of window. The right windows are worth the investment in terms of functionality and resale value. And if you do have a home with cheap, aluminum windows, this is a good place to spend some extra money to replace them. The expense will pay for itself in energy savings, and you will increase and protect the value of your home.

When choosing windows and doors, look through catalogs at the wide variety of styles. Research your home's architecture in books or over the Internet, and notice the type of window and door style used. Try to purchase windows that actually open, providing important ventilation. Go for substantial-looking windows and doors with thick sashes. When selecting windows with multiple panes, choose true divided light units with substantial muntins—the horizontal and vertical bars that frame the individual glass panes.

Also, mock up the outline of your windows and doors. Look at where the top of the opening hits the wall. Does it look low? Be sure the height of your windows and doors complements the space and doesn't diminish it. I encourage my clients to select the tallest windows and doors that look appropriate in the space. This helps the room feel bigger and grander as it keeps the eye up. Transom windows can also be placed over windows and doors for the same effect.

When choosing color sashes on prefabricated doors and windows, or paint colors for your openings, consider both the interior and exterior. Do you want the sashes to blend with some element on the outside, complement some element on the inside, or both? Generally, there are many windows and doors in a home, so their color is important. Don't be afraid to select colors other than white. Color can enhance your windows and doors, giving them strength, presence, and personality.

This Wine Country living room, which holds Blomberg French doors that open in, provides an example of how doors can interfere with furniture placement. Out-swinging doors provide greater flexibility in placing furniture and can make a room feel larger.

Strategically Placed Openings

When determining the placement of openings, again it is critical to consider both the exterior and interior of the structure. Let's start with the exterior. Look around the site and surrounding area. Where there is a view of anything pleasing (such as water, land, mountains, trees, a skyline, hillside, garden, bridge, beautiful building, monument, pool, patio, deck, sculpture, fountain, or birdbath) or the potential to put something pleasing, there should be an opening oriented toward it. I can't tell you how many homes I've walked into where this principle was overlooked. Other considerations for placing windows, doors, or skylights are the direction the opening faces, the climate you are in, and the sun and wind exposure of each direction.

If you live in a very sunny climate and can afford the extra expense, you may want to consider using Low-E glass in your windows, doors, and skylights. It allows the light in while blocking some of the harmful ultraviolet rays that can damage wood, rugs, and fabrics.

For existing doors without Low-E protection, the protective films made by 3M and other companies have been significantly improved in the past few years. If selected and applied properly they can be very helpful in taming the sun's rays while remaining virtually invisible. Of course, window treatments such as curtains, blinds, and shades can be the best defense against damage and fading from the sun.

IF YOU LIVE IN A VERY SUNNY CLIMATE AND CAN AFFORD THE EXTRA EXPENSE, YOU MAY WANT TO CONSIDER USING LOW-E GLASS IN YOUR WINDOWS, DOORS, AND SKYLIGHTS.

Now let's take a look at the placement of openings and their relationship to a structure's interior. The size and placement of these very important bones is key in making a room feel warm or cold, light or dark, open and airy, alive or stagnant, welcoming or depressing. In addition, just as when considering the exterior, windows or doors that face a beautiful view can create a primary or secondary focal point in the *interior* of a room, which should be considered when arranging furniture. Strategically placed openings can also make a room feel much larger and allow the energy to flow. Installing a set of French doors at the end of a stagnant dining room or in a bedroom that feels closed off can make a huge difference in how the room feels. Connecting a room to a garden, deck, or patio can add light and amplify it significantly. Even if the doors do not open to a walkable area, you can still create an opening by swinging the doors to the inside and running a railing across the opening. This is common in European homes as well as in many hotel rooms.

Small mahogany casement windows open to connect to the outdoors and let in air and light, but are raised to provide privacy and wall space for this intimate family room.

FACING PAGE: Pitched lines of an angled window emulate the peak of the Transamerica Building in San Francisco's skyline. This small pent-room on the top floor of a loft-like space on Nob Hill feels huge and wondrous with the City by the Bay as its backdrop.

ABOVE: Waters run deep outside this contemporary yet traditional window overlooking boats on a bay. The presence and placement of the horizontal band keep the window from looking too contemporary and create a smaller pane sized for opening, yet it doesn't interfere with the view. The window's rich mahogany detail complements the elegant old-world furnishings.

The small, dark entry of Clorinda, with its solid front door, was brightened and expanded by installing an old, recycled door with a window rescued from a salvage yard. The door was retro-fitted with tempered glass, custom-built jambs, and weather stripping to bring it up to today's standards.

Door Swing Options

Whenever possible, however, I prefer doors that open out so they don't interfere with furniture placement inside a room. They also make a room feel larger. If you prefer doors that open in or must choose them for functional reasons, at least consider in advance your furniture placement, allowing room for the window and door swings. Something else to think about is whether your home has any openings large enough to accept a big item such as a sectional sofa, a piano, or a Christmas tree—items you may not even own now. A six-foot slider or pair of French doors installed in a room where a window could have gone might have furniture in front of it 364 days a year, but, oh, how you'll be glad you have it on that 365th day!

When buying new windows or doors, be sure they won't leak if opened out. Most manufacturers today have remedied this problem with interlocking weather stripping and higher thresholds, but it's always a good idea to ask. And, when planning for doors or windows that open out, make sure they don't open into a walkway or other area that might prove dangerous. Sliding doors and double-hung windows don't impact the outside space and are a good choice if exterior space is limited.

Consider which new door is the *active* one on sets of French doors and double sliders—the

The black metal frames of these sliding glass doors ground and complement this colorful contemporary living room. The light-weight aluminum doors were eventually replaced with Blomberg doors, which are similar in style but have heavier aluminum frames and give more of a quality look and feel.

RIGHT: Who says you need a view? The once-frosted old window that opens to the inside blocked the sunshine from the brick light well in the entry of this city loft. The frosted panes were replaced with clear ones, the light well painted red, and a fern placed on the unused, black high-gloss trash chute. The result was an opening that expanded the feeling of the entry, let in light, and brought a touch of nature to this urban dwelling.

BELOW: To get double duty from your existing windows and doors, use strategically located mirrors. The large mirror placed opposite the window across the room reflects light, and at first glance looks like another window.

This windowless entry gets enlightened by the adjoining stairwell opening, which appears as an unusually-shaped window reflected in the overscaled mirror.

30 Openings of All Kinds

ABOVE: This relatively small, windowless dining room, dominated by a large table and chairs, is expanded and amplified by the opening to the sea. Doors swing open to a deck that extends the space, beckoning guests outside and bringing in light and a sense of expansiveness.

LEFT: Only partly visible in the photo, a ridge beam skylight flanks either side of the rustic, recycled beam in this country-style home and balances the light in the room. The black metal skylight was framed with wood slats, then painted to soften its modern feel and to help it blend with the newly paneled wood ceiling.

one that locks and unlocks the unit and opens first. You'll want to be sure the active door has ample space to swing without hitting furniture, whether it opens in or out. Considering which is the active door can also be useful in furniture placement. If never opened, the inactive door can serve as a window against which furniture can be placed.

Whenever possible, it's best if the interior and exterior floor surfaces are at the same level where they meet at a door's threshold. This makes for a smoother transition and is easier and safer to navigate. Using the same flooring materials indoors and out, or at least those of similar colors and textures, creates the smoothest transition.

Old versus New

I love old windows and doors. Your local building department may, however, dictate the necessity of using double-paned glass, which may prohibit the use of recycled openings. But if you are allowed to use them, you can have a lot of fun finding old windows and doors at salvage yards. They are generally inexpensive to buy but expensive to install, because they usually need to be retro-fitted with custom jambs, weather stripping, and hardware. The cost is probably still below that of new units, but they might not seal, protect, or operate as well as high-quality new windows. For me, using old windows and doors was worth it when we remodeled Clorinda, but you, of course, have to make the choice that's right for you.

Existing Windows and Doors

If you are not building a new home, remodeling, or adding or replacing windows and doors, consider your existing openings. Do they let in light and connect to the outdoors? Are they covered with heavy shutters or window treatments? Do they contain frosted glass? It is fairly inexpensive to have frosted glass replaced with clear glass. If privacy is a factor, consider sheer or woven shades, which offer privacy during the day, yet still let in light and allow views to the outdoors. If the view is of an adjacent building, place a plant or a window box outside to draw the eye to something pleasing. Heavier drapes or shades can be used in conjunction with the sheers and wovens to provide privacy at night.

OPPOSITE: An old French train station clock keeps time in this once-contemporary light well. An Italian country home takes on an old-world look with the placement of recycled, sandblasted, and stained beams below the skylight to soften its dramatic opening to the kitchen below.

One of my favorite ways to amplify windows and doors in a home is with mirrors. Mirrors that are strategically placed to reflect openings not only expand the feel of a room and increase light, but can also look like another window or door at first glance. I call this "the smoke and mirrors trick," and I use it liberally in darker homes to create views and light everywhere.

Sizzling Skylights

Skylights usually look contemporary, which is fine in a modern home but doesn't really work in a traditional setting. When I am trying to create a more classic look and feel in a home, I will frame skylights with wood and also cover their cold, black metal bars with wood. Whenever possible, I use ridge beam skylights, which are skylights placed on both sides of a beam in a room with a pitched ceiling or an exposed beam that runs above a flat ceiling. They have the advantage of balancing the light on both sides of a beam. My favorite treatment of skylights is to paint the well and surrounding walls a warm, nurturing color, and as the sun streams down the skylight's well, the entire room is bathed in an enticing glow.

It pays to give serious thought to your skylight placements. A skylight facing west, for example, might be just the thing a room needs for extra light and warmth; or, on the contrary it can make a room unbearably hot and damage the furnishings. You always want to buy high-quality skylights, preferably with Low-E glass, especially in sunny areas. And finally, whenever possible, install skylights that open either manually or electrically. They create great ventilation and are especially important in a bathroom to release steam and moisture.

FINDING THE RIGHT WINDOWS, DOORS, AND SKYLIGHTS AND PLACING THEM APPROPRIATELY IS ONE WAY TO INCORPORATE GREAT BONES OR ARCHITECTURAL CHARACTER INTO YOUR HOME.

Openings in your walls and ceilings can expand and light up your living space, help your home work with rather than against the weather, connect you to nature and fresh air, and enhance your architectural statement. Finding the right windows, doors, and skylights and placing them appropriately is one way to incorporate great bones or architectural character into your home.

Patrick Jackson, of JDA Architects & Planners in Portland, Oregon, designed the wonderful arched sky roof over a hallway in this contemporary home. The walls and floors below are bathed in warm, earthy colors to reflect the light and produce a radiant glow.

BEAMS & Lintels

"Raise high the roof beam, carpenters."

—J.D. SALINGER

FACING PAGE: The structural supports, or rafters, in this contemporary country loggia are made of fir that has been sandblasted and turned a rich terracotta color over time. Decorative rectangular lintels of aged white oak were installed in the loggia's passageways between richly plastered walls. The square lintel over the double doors at the end of the corridor, which visually raises the height of the opening, is made of the same aged white oak.

WORKING WITH STRUCTURAL ELEMENTS such as beams and lintels is one of the best ways of adding character to a home. Beams and lintels are horizontal framing members designed to support various structures in a home. Whether functional or decorative, when left exposed these big boys make a powerful statement, adding strength and substance to a structure. But due to the soaring cost of wood in today's construction, more and more steel and engineered woods, such as glulams, are being used, and there's good reason to hide them behind walls and ceilings.

If you are building a home, you have the opportunity to expose or incorporate attractive structural beams and lintels in a way that supports your overall design theme. With a remodel, you also have the opportunity to expose structural elements; however, it is important to determine first if they are worth exposing! If a house's framework is not visually appealing, it can be impractical in terms of time and money to make it so. Of course, attractiveness is a relative term, as evidenced by the exposed framing, conduit, ductwork, and pipes you now frequently see in living spaces (typically lofts) located in industrial buildings.

In my experience in working both with new construction and remodels, it is often easier, less time consuming, and less expensive to simply add decorative beams and lintels that have the look of structural elements but are not actually load bearing.

Adding Decorative Beams

Beams lend themselves to both traditional and contemporary architecture. The type of beam and its decorative treatment help to set the tone for how a room feels and the design statement it makes. Decorative beams can change an unsubstantial-looking box into a fabulous room with rich architectural features. They can transform a room with a pitched, drywall ceiling—that feels stark and contemporary—into a room that feels traditional or rustic, with warmth and texture. I add beams to rooms to create strength, character, and interest, particularly rooms without a lot of trim or moldings.

In determining the size and shape of decorative beams, the scale of the room and other existing structural elements should be considered. If there is a large ridge beam and you would like decorative rafters to run perpendicular to it, then first consider the size of the ridge beam. The rafters should be smaller than the main beam but possibly the same shape. My motto: when in doubt, mock it up. Create a section of a beam or rafter out of a piece of cardboard or wood, and then tack it to the ceiling. Look at it from all angles. Try various sizes and shapes until you achieve the look you want.

FACING PAGE: Patrick Jackson, JDA Architects and Planners of Portland, Oregon, designed these structural beams in this contemporary home. The beams are made of engineered wood called a glulam. Once installed, the glulam was wrapped in drywall, covered with a heavily textured plaster, and painted green to match the Blomberg doors, posts, and windows.

GENERAL FRAMING COMPONENTS

Beam—A horizontal or diagonal framing member spanning an open space, designed to carry a load from a set of joists or a roof.

Lintel—Exposed horizontal crosspiece over a window or door that carries the weight of the structure above it.

Rafter—A beam that slopes from the ridge of a roof to the eaves to serve as support for the roof.

Truss—A framework of girders, struts, bars, and other pieces used to support a roof or other load-bearing elements.

Framework—The skeletal structure of a building.

Header—The horizontal structural member immediately above an opening.

Engineered Wood—A wood product composed of wood veneers glued together under heat and pressure.

Ridge Beam—A horizontal member that serves as a support in the highest point of the roof structure.

RIGHT: This country kitchen is crowned with a massive beam that was required to hold the two sides of the structure together. At its core, the beam is a glulam that has been wrapped with sandblasted fir. The large metal pot rack gives the structural element double duty.

FACING PAGE: The decorative beams give an old-world feeling to this Wine Country living room. The old beams, recycled from a local hotel, were first sandblasted to soften the corners and add texture and then coated with a lustrous brown oil-based stain.

Beams are typically square or rectangular in shape. Solid wood beams, which are usually made of fir, can be purchased at a local lumberyard in 2-inch increments of width and height. For example, 4 x 4-, 4 x 6-, 4 x 8-, 6 x 6-, 6 x 8-, and 6 x 10-inch beams can be bought in varying lengths. However, beams come rough cut, which means they have been through a band saw that takes approximately ¼ -inch off their diameter. Or, they may have been surfaced with a band saw and planer, reducing their diameter by approximately ½-inch. So, for example, a rough cut 4 x 4-inch beam actually measures 3 ¾ x 3 ¾-inches, whereas a surfaced 4 x 4-inch beam measures 3 ½ x 3 ½-inches.

Generally, the largest beams most lumberyards carry are 6 inches x 12 inches x 20 feet long. Larger beams than this usually have to be special ordered. An alternative to buying new beams is to consider using old or reclaimed beams, which often can be found in very large sizes at salvage yards or salvage lumberyards and are relatively inexpensive compared to new ones. I love using old building materials. They have great character and patina and can add so much richness to an interior. But be careful—old lumber often contains nails and has been

Distressed and faux-painted 8 x 8-inch beams soften the raised inset ceiling of this European country family room. The decorative beams were faux painted a lighter wood color to prevent the fir from turning dark over time from exposure to light. In addition, the softer color of the beams, as opposed to heavy dark brown beams, helps make the ceiling feel higher.

The ceiling of this rustic California country dining room is embellished with old, distressed decorative beams that add texture and dimension while complementing the hand-built stone walls.

known to chew up even the toughest saw blades. I recommend using a metal detector—a quality lumberyard will sell them—to find nails and remove them from old beams before you use them.

Whether old or new, solid wood beams are always preferable to glulams, but they can be expensive. If your budget is limited, decorative beams can be built out of 2 inch x whatever width and length you want the beam to be. When building beams, I prefer to miter the joints to form perfect right angles at the corners, but be aware that these mitered joints can open over time with exposure to hot and cold temperatures. Use kiln-dried, vertical-grain fir along with a very sharp saw blade to keep the mitered joints from separating. Talk to your contractor as early in the building process as possible about your intent to use decorative beams so that he or she can install the proper framing to support them.

RIGHT: To bring this one-hundred-year-old cottage back to its former self, we put 1 x 12-inch pine planks on the once-contemporary drywalled ceiling, and then installed an old beam to cover the joint where the horizontal and angled planks met.

BELOW: A special-order 4 x 10-inch rough-cut beam provides the primary horizontal support for this redwood arbor. The big boy is topped by a series of 2 x 8-inch rough-cut smaller redwood beams that have been fashioned to harmonize with the painted border detail on the stucco wall.

Transforming Openings with Lintels

Lintels, or exposed headers, can transform an opening and lend themselves to a variety of architectural styles. Structural (load-bearing) lintels are made from a substantial piece of steel, wood, or stone. You often see them in old European structures over windows and doors, and in adobe construction in Mexico and the Southwest. Lintels are usually seen above windows, doors, or passageways that have no trim and are bordered by substantial walls.

Decorative lintels look the part but don't carry any weight and can be installed once the walls are framed and even drywalled. I use decorative lintels to soften hard-edged drywalled openings between rooms or on plaster openings that look contemporary where a more rustic feeling is desired.

To raise the height and soften the feeling of a contemporary drywalled passageway between this elegant rustic dining and living room, a decorative lintel was added. An old recycled 6 x 8-inch painted beam from a salvage yard was hollowed out and slipped over the upper wall of the opening, creating interest and texture, while adding height to the opening.

There are several ways to install decorative lintels. The first method requires plastered walls and is done during the plastering stage. The lintel is installed at the top of the opening, slightly inset from the corners of the walls, and then the top and side joints between the lintel and the wall are plastered. If done properly, this will result in a lintel that looks embedded and original to the structure. If your walls are already plastered or drywalled, then install the lintel as tightly as possible at the top of the opening and slightly inset from the adjoining walls.

RIGHT: This structural lintel adorns the entryway of a 1920s Mediterranean home. Decorative corbels and a stone architectural fragment were added for embellishment. To create a more rustic feeling, the lintel and corbels were enhanced with a rich color and pronounced knots by decorative painter Arno Cornillion.

FACING PAGE: A distressed and painted glulam supports the ridge of this newly pitched ceiling, while 3 x 6-inch recycled beams add character and texture to the once 8-foot-high drywalled ceiling. The opening from the living room into the small entry is softened by the addition of a 6 x 6-inch painted and distressed fir beam, which simulates a lintel.

Another method is to cut and hollow out either an old or new beam to the length and width of the opening. Then push the beam up and over the outside of the top of the opening, actually encasing the lower section of the wall above the passageway. If plastering the surrounding walls, be sure to plaster over the edge of the lintel to give it an embedded look.

This latter method has the added advantage of making the passageway appear higher. The other methods described will actually decrease the height of the finished opening. This should be considered when deciding which method of installation to use. During the framing process, the height of an opening can be raised so that the installation of the lintel will not make the passageway too low. I like to create dramatic passageways between rooms and always attempt to raise the eye, making grand openings, particularly in conjunction with higher ceilings. There's nothing worse than ruining the look of grand, high ceilings with low passageways that bring the eye down and diminish the room.

In terms of materials, I have always used wooden decorative lintels. They are lighter and easier to install than stone or steel. Lintels can be rectangular or square. Again, remember the mock-up motto. Fashion a section of a lintel out of a piece of cardboard—or your contractor can usually do it quickly out of scrap lumber—and tack it to the opening. Look at it from across the room. And remember, good design repeats itself. If there are other structural or decorative architectural elements in the room, such as beams or rafters, the lintels should correspond in scale, look, and feel.

ABOVE: A 2-foot x 8-inch rectangular plank of old oak gives definition to the opening in this California country bathroom. Mounting the faux lintel and vintage corbels provided additional strength and contrast in color and texture to the plastered walls.

FACING PAGE: For this cottage bathroom, simply adding a length of distressed and painted fir to simulate a lintel converted an ordinary drywalled opening into a strong and unique passageway.

When to Sandblast, Stain, Paint, Plaster, or Faux Finish

Beams and lintels create substantial bones, but the decorative treatment used on them makes an impact, either enhancing a room or detracting from the overall design. It's important to know the options in terms of treatment of these prominent elements.

Old beams or lintels, which are often caked with years of dirt, rust, or paint, may call for sandblasting. Sandblasting can remove these built-up layers and return the pieces to their original condition. It also works well on new beams where you might want to soften the edges and achieve a more rustic look.

An unattractive drywalled beam gains definition and strength through faux finishing. The uncomplementary structural element was enlarged and painted to look like an old fir beam, turning a negative into a positive and adding substance to this remodeled *pied à terre*.

The ideal time to sandblast is before beams are installed, but the process can be done to beams and lintels already in place. Be prepared—it makes quite a mess, with lots of dust and debris everywhere. Also be aware that sandblasting old beams can remove the aged patina, actually making them look new.

If you decide to sandblast, be sure it is the first thing done to the beams or lintels. You may not need to do anything else. Sandblasted beams and lintels can be beautiful left natural without staining, but some woods like fir, cherry, redwood, and mahogany change color over time with exposure to light. Check with a decorative painter, cabinet finisher, or paint store to learn what can be done to prevent these color changes if not desired. There are some good UV sealers on the market that cut out ultraviolet light.

After sandblasting, the color of the beams or lintels may need to be adjusted by staining. Always test the stain options on raw wood first. It is a good idea to talk to a professional painter or expert at a paint store about what type of stain to use—oil-based or water-based—and what type of sealer, if any, is recommended. Beams and lintels are generally not touched once they are installed, so they do not have to be sealed; however, sometimes it might be desirable to flatten the shine left by staining. Some stains do produce a strong sheen, which a sealer can help to remedy. Again, ask your painter.

If there are hardwood floors and stained or natural wood cabinets in rooms where beams and lintels appear, the color of all these elements should harmonize and complement one another. For example, with clear-coated redwood floors, the beams or lintels might need a touch of red or warmth to complement the floors. It is best not to match them exactly—it looks too contrived.

Another decorative option is to paint beams and lintels, making it easier to control the sheen. Don't forget to prime the beams and lintels before painting, especially if they contain knots, and

> **Sandblasting**—The process of smoothing, shaping, and cleaning a hard surface such as wood, metal, or masonry to create a bondable or decorative surface by forcing solid particles or compressed air across that surface at high speeds.

you don't want the knots to show. Knots will eventually bleed through the paint unless a primer is used.

If you are using plaster on the beams or lintels, you can achieve a variety of looks, from contemporary to rustic to elegant. It depends on the type of plaster, its sheen, and the method of application. Most decorative painters do plaster work. Ask to see samples of various plaster finishes so you get the right look and feel.

I am a big believer in using a skilled decorative (also called "faux" or "artistic") painter who can make anything look like something it's not. You can take an unattractive glulam or a funky old beam with water stains, nail holes, and pieces gouged out of it to a good decorative painter, include some clear instructions or a picture of what you want the beam to look like, and *voilà!* Your dream beam appears.

These treatments can make your home's new or old bones—structural or decorative beams and lintels—create the design statement you want, but it takes research and trying out different options.

Look through design books for different beam and lintel treatments. Wherever you go—restaurants, shops, public spaces—notice if there are any exposed structural elements. How are they treated? Do they contrast or blend into the surrounding area? Are they smooth or textured, rustic or elegant? Remember, you can always mock up a finish, which will help you better visualize the effect a given treatment will have on a room. Sense in your gut what you like, then create these good bones. Your rooms will become so much more interesting with the "big boys" around.

> **Glulam**—Short for "glued and laminated structural timber," glulam is among the most versatile of the engineered wood products. It can be shaped into forms ranging from straight beams to complex curved members for a wide variety of construction applications.

IF YOU ARE USING PLASTER ON THE BEAMS OR LINTELS, YOU CAN ACHIEVE A VARIETY OF LOOKS, FROM CONTEMPORARY TO RUSTIC TO ELEGANT.

No one is the wiser that this once unappealing structural glulam was transformed into a richly beautiful beam, complete with color variation and a sampling of knots. The faux-finished beam creates perfect harmony with the old fir stairs and flooring in this San Francisco loft.

Two new engineered lumber beams were installed in this old converted garage to support the structure for the lobby of a Wine Country bed and breakfast inn. Artist Shawn Man Roland distressed and painted the unattractive laminated plywood elements to look like old, rustic beams in tones that complement the cabinet detail and floor tiles.

FAT ARCHES
& Deep Niches

"Architecture is art
you can walk
through."

—DAN RICE

FACING PAGE: Character and good bones
abound in this old Mediterranean home
with a 15-inch-deep brick arch that
invites you into the family room and
then surprises you with a pointed niche
inside the arch. Rubbing a richer tone
of the wall color onto the perimeter of
the arch and niche accents the strong yet
graceful architectural detail.

IT WAS DURING THE REMODEL OF CLORINDA that I first
learned about the importance of fat walls—walls that are framed
thicker than the typical 2 x 4 construction. Fat-wall framing not
only offers opportunities to create elegant, substantial openings
between rooms but also provides the option to create fat arches
and deep niches. I found that both arches (usually curved con-
structions that span an opening) and niches (recesses in walls)
create really good bones or architectural details in a room.

In addition to the use of fat walls with lintels, arches create
elegant and graceful passageways between rooms. And they add
another component that lintels don't; they bring the softness of
curved lines into the design and architecture of what might
otherwise be a straight-lined room.

Why Fat Arches Are Lovelier

Arches can be used many ways in a home—with windows,
doors, soffits, and niches; in cabinet design; and even over garage
doors. But whenever arches are incorporated into a wall, the wall
and arch need to be fat. As I stated earlier, when there is a significant passageway or opening between rooms that does not have a
door, the walls of the opening should look substantial, especially

Arches that span openings between rooms should be fat, preferably a minimum of 8 inches deep. The bordering fat wall adds a sense of quality to Clorinda, while the graceful elliptical arch softens the surrounding straight lines of the structure.

FAT WALLS NEED BE CREATED ONLY WHERE MAJOR PASSAGEWAYS EXIST.

walls without trim. Why? Because passageways between rooms without doors or trim provide an opportunity to actually see the end or cross section of a wall. With typical framing and drywall, this cross section is 4 inches thick. Now, that's a skimpy looking wall, and I have been in many high-end homes that have this regrettable problem. Skimpy walls and arches look cheap and unsubstantial. They degrade the feeling of a structure, insinuating that all the walls are thin and that the house is inexpensively built. Fat walls do the opposite. They create the impression that all the walls are thick and substantial, lending more of a quality feeling to the entire house. Fat walls need be created only where major passageways exist. In Clorinda, we built only one fat wall in the whole house, but the feeling of strength and quality it exuded pervaded the entire structure.

When creating fat walls and arches to enhance major passageways, I think the framing should be a minimum of 7 to 8 inches thick. Once the framing is done and the drywall is up, joint compound, or mud, is added, which can be applied smoothly (called smooth wall) or with a variety of textures. Try to avoid having texture blown onto walls or using a mudding technique called skip-troweling. These are two of the least expensive ways to texture drywall, and they look it. They lack both character and the quality of a hand-applied texture. Custom plastering can add some slight thickness to walls and offers a wonderful variety of textures. But it can be expensive. Always ask for texture or plaster samples from your contractor before choosing a finish.

Be sure when planning a fat arch to mock up the line of it by cutting out a piece of cardboard in the shape of the proposed opening and putting it in place, leaving a substantial amount of wall on either side and on top of the arch. In designing the shape of an arch in a home that already has

COMMONLY USED TYPES OF ARCHES

Elliptical Arch—A flattened arch designed by joining a quarter circle to each end of a false ellipse.

Flat Arch—An arch that has a horizontal top surface, with a span of up to 6 feet.

Pointed Arch—Arch produced by two curves that meet in the center, forming a point.

Round Arch—Arch in the shape of a semicircle.

Tudor Arch—A triangular arch with soft curves at the bottom two corners.

Niches can be both decorative and functional. This 6-inch-deep niche in Clorinda's kitchen, set into a fat-framed wall, is finished with recycled French paver tiles and an old fir shelf. The niche smartly serves as a backsplash for the cooktop and a display area for a collection of French pottery.

arches, it's best to repeat the shape of the existing ones. When I introduce arches as part of new construction, I prefer to repeat the same shape elsewhere in the home.

My favorite shapes are elliptical and semicircular arches, and I sometimes use a combination of both. Whenever I incorporate a curved arch into a wall, I try to repeat the same shape throughout the project. I use arches at the top of bookcases, in cabinet doors, in transom windows, in soffits over bathroom or kitchen counters, and in niches. In European-style or old-world style projects, I might use elliptical arches in walls and round arches in niches. There are no rules. Always mock up shapes when in doubt of how an arch will look and what size it should be. Arches and niches should have a substantial amount of wall around them and should be in scale with the room and other structural elements.

Choosing Materials

Arches make strong statements in a variety of materials—stone, brick, wood, stucco, plaster, drywall, or a combination.

The simplest and least expensive way to create an arched opening is with wood framing and drywall, which can look great as long as the arch is kept fat and the wall texture attractive. The wall finish can vary from a smooth wall, for a more elegant, refined look, to a rough texture, for a more rustic look or the look of old plaster. A good faux finisher or even a highly skilled drywaller can achieve these looks. Plastering the drywall can add a different feel and texture but is definitely more expensive. Plastering takes from one to two coats and can be applied raw. It can either be painted or faux painted to achieve different effects or applied with integral color where the color pigment has actually been added to the plaster. The latter is

Good design repeats itself. The arched plaster soffit above the bathroom counter, glow-lit by sconces, adds an elegant touch to this California country bathroom. The curves at the bottom of the cabinet doors mimic the shape of the arch, a detail that reinforces the design concept for the room.

usually the most expensive plaster application. The choice of plaster texture and technique depends again on the look or feeling you desire. Plaster is well suited for many varied looks, including rustic, formal, old-world, and contemporary projects. A plasterer or faux finisher can provide various texture samples. Note that plaster walls are difficult to retouch; painted walls are much easier. Often, to retouch a section or small area of a plaster wall, the entire wall must be replastered.

Start observing wall treatments and arches wherever you go—in restaurants, design-oriented stores, antique shops, friends' homes, old houses, museums, and new and model homes. When picking a look for your walls and arches, always respect your architecture and make choices that complement the style of your home.

Arches of varying shapes, sizes, and materials add old-world charm to this Wine Country patio. Antique bricks rim the curve of the bread oven in the center of the outdoor kitchen, while arched openings in the stucco wall provide views to the vineyards. Hand-built stone walls support softly arched transom windows above French doors.

Small and large 8-inch-deep arched openings provide views and a passageway to the adjoining patio. The small arch is anchored and extended by a limestone slab. The larger arched opening is graced by a pair of curved concrete elements placed end to end to provide an interesting architectural detail above the archway.

RIGHT: We replaced a closet in the small entryway of Clorinda with a large-arched niche, which expands the space, adding depth and perspective. The textured drywalled niche was faux painted to give the look of old plaster. A recessed low-voltage light fixture creates a glow, while a mirror reflects the outdoors.

FACING PAGE: This fat wall with its equally fat arch was created by double framing the typical 2 x 4-inch wall with 2 x 8-inch materials and then wrapping it with 1/2-inch drywall to create an 8 1/2-inch-deep wall.

Expanding Space with Large Niches

Niches come in all shapes and sizes and are not always simply decorative. They can be functional as well by creating additional space in a home.

At Clorinda, our front door opened to a tiny entryway, with a coat closet directly across from the front door. I hated walking into a closet door when I entered the house, so I eliminated the closet and created a niche in its place. The niche is several feet deep, so the walls are fat. I arched the top and installed a low-voltage light to illuminate the space. The resulting niche expands the entrance of the house, creating a warm, welcoming space for an antique table and a carved, painted mirror. The niche not only adds a sense of space and beauty but is functional as well. It creates a spot to collect keys and do a last-minute mirror check before walking out the door.

These large niches that encompass floor space can be used in many ways—to expand an entry, hold a buffet table in a dining room, contain a window seat, display a piece of sculpture, or even hold a vanity in a bathroom.

FACING PAGE: This elegant round entryway niche was created by recessing a 7-foot x 4-foot x 8-inch deep section of wall back into a kitchen pantry. The niche and molding detail on the rim are made of hand-applied plaster, which was then faux painted to achieve a glowing patina. The unusual plaster elements bordering the niche, originally installed in the dining room of this remodeled 1920s Mediterranean-style home, were placed on either side of the recess to create drama and interest in the entry.

ABOVE: Patrick Jackson, JDA Architects and Planners of Portland, Oregon, designed three small but deep arched wall niches to add architectural interest to this rustic dining room. The niches, which extend through to the exterior of the home, were backed with a golden alabaster that glows when the sun shines through.

An Italian country home is embellished with this 15 x 30 x 6-inch niche anchored by a ¾-inch-thick slab of old gold limestone. The apricot-colored stucco niche provides the perfect place to display this antique icon collected during the homeowners' travels.

Creating Drama and Purpose with Small, Deep Niches

As typically seen in many spec homes today, very tall, narrow, and shallow niches create drama, but to my eye do not necessarily make a positive design statement. Just as fat walls and arches make a passageway look substantial and contribute to an overall feeling of quality in a home, deep wall niches do the same.

Deep wall niches provide perspective, subtly making a room look and feel larger. A deep niche creates the opportunity to display a treasured object or create interesting lighting effects, while adding architectural character to a room. Niches, like arches, come in many shapes—square, pointed, rounded, or slightly curved, like the top of an oval. They can be created in almost any depth, depending on the framing of the wall in which they are set. If you have a decorative object such as a sculpture or a vase that you want to highlight, you might plan your niche with the size of your object in mind. Work out the framing parameters during the planning stage of a remodel or new construction. The height and width of a niche are easy to incorporate into a wall, but the depth can be more difficult. I think niches ideally should be at least five inches deep to look authentic. You can cheat with this measurement by placing a wood or stone base in the bottom of the niche extending past the wall—something like a window sill—to make the niche look deeper.

Wall niches can be made from a variety of materials in an assortment of shapes. For an old-world look, they can be made of stone, or they can be lined with mirrors for a more contemporary look. When constructed of drywall, niches can be painted a different color than the wall, given a contrasting texture, or enhanced with an unusual decorative treatment such as wall flowering.

In terms of lighting niches, there are several methods to consider. I prefer using low-voltage lighting whenever possible, as I find that it most effectively simulates the look of natural light. One low-voltage light placed at the top of a niche will usually light the area. Or, you can place the light source several feet away in the ceiling and aim it at the niche, but this does create a shadow. Again, it depends on the look you are trying to achieve. If I want an authentic old-world look, I will not put a light in the niche; obviously an ancient niche would not have contained an electric light. And, depending on the feeling I'm going for I might want to light the niche from the outside to play with shadow. Candles are another great way to light niches. They create a warm and romantic atmosphere.

Finding Your Niche

How can you incorporate niches into the structure of your home? What walls or openings could you transform? What objects could you showcase? What other purpose would the niches serve? Look through design books and magazines for ideas, and plan for niches early in your building or remodeling process. Discuss their size and placement with your contractor. Mock them up with a piece of cardboard. Repeat their shape in other elements in your home, such as cabinets or soffits. Create fat arches that harmonize with your deep niches, exuding the look of quality construction in your home. Be creative, take risks, and have fun using these architectural elements to add pizzazz, romance, and drama to your rooms.

This graceful arched niche was beautifully embellished by artist Zdravko Terziev with handsome wallflowering, the art of squeezing plaster from a pastry tube to form decorative details. Candles sit on a shelf made of honed and antiqued onyx, adding further embellishment while harmonizing with the contrasting wall and niche colors.

RIGHT: A dramatic arched soffit gives this master bathroom old-world ambiance, while encasing the vanity in its own elegant niche.

FACING PAGE: Architectural interest abounds in this elegant bathroom, which combines fat walls and a softly arched soffit to frame the bathtub. The deep-lighted niche provides ample room for a lovely statue, while the window treatment mimics the room's sensuous, glowing curves.

Uncommon
COLUMNS,
Posts, & Pilasters

"Consider the
momentous event in
architecture when
the wall parted and
the column
became."

—LOUIS KAHN

AMONG THE BEST BONES a room can have are vertically dramatic columns, posts, and pilasters. I look for opportunities to install these fat boys whether I need them structurally or not. They add drama and architectural character to a room and serve a host of other purposes at the same time.

A quick definition of terms: Columns and posts are free-standing, while pilasters are engaged or embedded in a wall. All three can be made of wood, stone, concrete, metal, drywall, or fiberglass, as well as a number of other synthetic materials.

Columns, posts, and pilasters have been around forever. The Greeks and Romans used them abundantly in their architecture, and with good reason. They are relatively simple to install, lend themselves to any architectural style, provide structural support, create rooms without walls, give sturdy definition to a space, and add exciting architectural interest. They can also serve to bring the eye up to focus on a ceiling element or, with their tall vertical line, can even fool the eye to counteract a low-hung ceiling. I call this technique "using the vertical."

Why do I refer to these vertical elements as fat boys? Because the best of them are substantial looking. Like fat walls, fat columns give a feeling of quality and substance to a room. Although in modern construction vertical structural support is typically hidden within walls (it's cheaper and faster and takes

A 15-inch-diameter, antique redwood column found at a salvage yard for $50 makes an uncommon architectural statement in this '50s-era tract home.

less skill to build them that way), historically columns and posts were primarily used to provide support. Decorative columns and posts should look the part as well, and the same applies to pilasters. Ornamental pilasters have adorned classical architecture for ages, purely for the decorative effect, but these vertical elements should be fat if they're going to provide good bones or building blocks for your interior design.

Fat Boy Definitions

Column—A vertical support often resting on a base, consisting of a shaft and capital.

Post—A vertical member used to support a horizontal beam or lintel.

Pilaster—A vertical member projecting from a wall, with a base and capital.

Pillar—A vertical, noncircular masonry support.

Base—The elaboration at the bottom of a column, pillar, or pilaster.

Capital—The elaboration at the top of a column, pillar, or pilaster.

Shaft—The long, vertical part of a column between the base and capital.

Lathe—A machine used for shaping a piece of material by rotating it rapidly along its axis while pressing it against a fixed cutting or abrading tool.

Load-bearing—A structural element that supports the weight of other construction members.

Finger-joint—Narrow extensions of wood, resembling fingers, that are cut in the ends of two pieces of wood to interlock and form a joint.

Columns and posts can be round or square. However, columns are generally more decorative, with a base, shaft, and capital; posts are simpler, without a capital or base. Pilasters can be curved or flat, and, like columns, they often have a base, shaft, and capital as well.

Creating Rooms without Walls

It was during the remodel of Clorinda that I first used a column solely to add architectural interest. We removed a wall that separated the living room from the hallway, which fortunately was not load-bearing. Although structurally we did not need a column to support the beam that ran above where the wall once stood, I opted to place a decorative column under the beam just to add some drama.

The column did several things. It defined and separated the living room from the hallway, taking the place of the wall that once stood there, while

simultaneously combining the two spaces. It also provided a backdrop against which to place furniture. This surprised me. I pushed a big armchair up against it and the column backed it beautifully. It actually created an invisible line on which I placed a second armchair and, between the two chairs, a round table.

Getting the column to fit the space between the floor and the previously installed beam was easy. Artist John Hull simply built a beautiful base for the column and then added a layer to the top of the capital to make the old, silver fat boy fit perfectly.

ABOVE: Twelve-inch square columns with heavy bases embellish this large passageway to a playful seaside living room. The dramatic columns were changed from white, which matched the trim, to a deeper shade of the living room wall color, giving them definition and strength.

LEFT: A non-load-bearing wall separating the hallway from the living room was removed and replaced by an old redwood column found at a salvage yard. The column, which defined the two spaces, created an invisible line on which to place the living room furniture.

Column Creativity

Columns can also be used outside to provide structural support under arbors or gazebos or as decorative elements in a garden, but carefully consider the shape, size, and treatment of these fat boys when incorporating them into your outdoor rooms. Always respect the architecture you're working with, and sense what shape column would harmonize best—round or square. This is true when using columns indoors as well. If you have an existing column in your home, repeat its shape. I usually don't mix column shapes and keep them exclusively round or square throughout a structure.

ABOVE: Tapered 12-inch-diameter columns made of finger-jointed pine wrap around structural posts in this Wine Country dining room. The gessoed and faux-painted columns, which sit on the lower step leading to the adjacent hallway, define the space beautifully without the restriction of solid walls.

FACING PAGE: An inexpensive yet indestructible fiberglass column, fauxed to look like stone, wraps around the structural support for this terrace arbor and looks handsome and stately while defining the covered and uncovered sections of the outdoor room.

Round columns tend to feel a little more formal, lending themselves to more traditional architecture. However, as always, there are no rules and certainly there can be exceptions to this principle. What is true, once again, is that good design repeats itself, so look around you, or at your plans for a remodel or new home. Repeat elements that you see, or create new ones and repeat them again and again.

If you use a round column, you may want to incorporate curves elsewhere in the structure—in arches, windows, niches, or soffits—to reflect this style. If you incorporate square columns, then you want to repeat shapes that complement this more linear look. Of course, good design is made up of straight and curved lines, so somewhere in your design, throw in a few curves.

In terms of decorative treatment, columns (like beams) can be sandblasted, stained, painted, plastered, gessoed, or faux painted. It depends on what they're made of and the look you want to achieve. Round columns can be expensive and must be purchased ready-made, whereas square columns can easily be built out of basic stock materials and moldings. Round stone or brick columns are the most expensive in terms of material cost and installation. You can special order round limestone, marble, or concrete columns at your local tile and stone shop or on the Internet. Stone columns can also be purchased in semicircular pieces ranging from 14 to 24 inches wide that stack to form a round column. These pieces come in limestone, marble, and concrete and can be special ordered. Concrete or cast stone columns in both variations are significantly less expensive than marble or limestone. Round or square columns can also be made from bricks installed by a mason. They too can be wrapped around a structural support if required.

A series of fiberglass columns lines the edge of this deck backed by a hog-wire trellis. The low-cost columns coupled with inexpensive hog-wire create an unbeatable combo for embellishing a deck with a big bang for a small buck.

ABOVE: Artist Shawn Man Roland primed and distressed a shiny, white column to eliminate the smooth, glossy surface so a crackle medium would stick. Once the surface crackled, he taped off and painted the stripes and then antiqued the column, or rubbed stain into the cracks. A final sanding completed the transformation.

RIGHT: For an element of surprise, we added texture, golden vertical stripes, and a look of age to give drama and pizzazz to these simple structural elements. Who says classic white columns can't be made interesting?

Two bedrooms become one to create an expansive master suite in this California country home. A turned-fir column with a 14-inch diameter replaces the wall and supports the structure above to define the bedchamber from the sitting area.

Wood columns tend to be less expensive, easier to install, and more available. The most costly round wooden columns are custom ordered for size and shape and are made on a lathe. Less-expensive round columns made out of finger-jointed pine can be ordered in various sizes and shapes. However, before painting them, these columns must be coated in gesso or with two to three coats of primer to cover the joints. Round fiberglass columns are very inexpensive and great for use outdoors, as they are indestructible and require no maintenance. However, they always need some type of decorative finish to prevent them from looking inauthentic. They can be painted or fauxed to look like wood or stone, for example, and then coated with a tough exterior UV sealer.

I have found some of my favorite columns at salvage yards. Old wood, metal, or plaster columns have great patina and character and are easy to adjust in height by adding to the base or capital. That's one of the great things about columns. Their height can be changed with little difficulty as long as they have or look good with a base and capital. The tricky thing about round columns is determining what the appropriate diameter should be. Their girth is deceiving, and often what you

ABOVE: The 8 x 6-inch rectangular post was fabricated to simulate a structural support for the beam above. Both the drywalled beam and post were faux painted to look like the old fir that covers the stairs and floor of this eclectic *pied à terre*.

LEFT: A square steel post wrapped in drywall supports the corner of a waterfront living room. Plastering, faux paint, and layers of ornate molding transform the plain post into a handsome column.

The long hallway of this industrial loft gets visual relief from the strong concrete pilaster that stands resolutely to one side. The curve of the 14-inch-diameter post softens the linear space and is repeated in the track lighting and artwork on the walls.

LEFT: A 13-inch-wide flat antique pilaster adds definition between the Blomberg doors in this Wine Country living room, sharing the character of their age and the formality of their design with their new metal partners. The height of the pilasters relates well to the room's dimensions and serves as a surprising architectural detail.

FACING PAGE: An antique Corinthian capital made of pig iron adorns the top of a decorative pilaster that guards the entrance to this elegant French country kitchen. The 5 x 12-inch tapered pilaster was made from drywall and then plastered and faux painted by artist Shawn Man Roland to imitate the age of the capital.

think is a big enough diameter may turn out to be too small. I have made this mistake multiple times. It's hard to measure a round column with a tape measure and get a sense of it. Once again, when in doubt, mock one up!

Like round columns, square ones can be custom ordered in various materials and can also be found at salvage yards. Or, they can easily be built to wrap around a small or inauthentic-looking structural post. Stock building material can be added to the four sides of a structural member to create the size shaft that you want. If possible, I suggest using kiln-dried vertical grain fir and a very sharp saw blade to miter the corners of a square column shaft. This wood will not separate with fluctuations in temperature as other woods may. The base and capital of a square column can easily be made out of various sizes of wood and moldings; always take care to miter the corner joints at right angles. In addition, square columns can be made by wrapping drywall around a structural post. These can be plastered, painted, or fauxed with decorative moldings added to create the base and capital.

Unpredictable Posts

Square posts can be created with the same materials as columns but are less complicated, as they don't require a base or capital. These unadorned structural or decorative vertical elements usually lend themselves to more contemporary or rustic architecture. Although easier to create with less ornamentation, they have the same power that columns have. They can add dramatic structural or decorative bones to a room, and can create rooms without walls and define a space. They too should be fat—always looking sturdy and substantial.

SQUARE POSTS CAN BE CREATED WITH THE SAME MATERIALS AS COLUMNS BUT ARE LESS COMPLICATED, AS THEY DON'T REQUIRE A BASE OR CAPITAL.

Pilaster Appeal

Pilasters, which are vertical pillars embedded in a wall, can be structural or decorative. They can be square, rectangular, semicircular, or even flat, and they come in a variety of different materials. They, too, can be wrapped in wood or drywall and stained, plastered, or fauxed. Pilasters often have capitals or bases if a more traditional, rather than a contemporary feeling, is sought.

What sets pilasters apart from columns and posts is their ability to frame openings, including fireplaces and passageways. They can actually be wrapped around the end of a 4-inch framed wall and instantly make the wall look fat. I love using pilasters in this way as an alternative to double framing walls. They not only make walls appear substantial, but they add a decorative element as well. Pilasters used in this manner are typically made of wood and molding materials. They are easy to mock up, build, and embellish in a variety of architectural styles and make great structural and decorative supports for pediments.

If you want to cover unattractive structural elements in your home or embellish your rooms with these vertical fat boys, mock up a replica of a column, post, or pilaster. Determine the correct size, shape, and material you want to use. Consider looking in salvage yards for old columns, posts, or pilasters or creating them out of wood, concrete, or drywall. Think outside the box. Can you remove a wall and put a column in its place? Can you embellish an opening with columns or pilasters? Can you make a long hallway more interesting by adding posts or pilasters? Go on a mission to notice these vertical architectural elements wherever you go. You will be surprised by what you see and how these fat boys can add exceptionally good bones to your rooms.

These handsome pilasters do the job! Architect Dick Hunt, of Hunt Hale Jones Architects in San Francisco, framed this opening with substance and elegance, making the 2 x 4-inch walls appear fat, while they simultaneously support the overriding pediment, making the opening appear higher and grander.

Powerful MOLDINGS
& *Diverse Railings*

> "True ornament
> is not a matter
> of prettifying
> externals. It is
> organic with the
> structure it adorns,
> whether a person,
> a building,
> or a park."
>
> —FRANK LLOYD
> WRIGHT

FACING PAGE: The walls were painted a bold persimmon to accentuate the chair rail and doorway molding in this converted French laundry in San Francisco. Painting the walls with flat paint and the moldings with satin, which has a low sheen, creates a contrast in luminosity. We might have used semigloss paint for the moldings, except that here, the wood is decades old and a higher sheen would have revealed many imperfections.

MOLDINGS AND RAILINGS can create fabulous ornamentation in a home if you recognize their power and use it effectively. These two diverse powerhouses can be used sparingly or effusively to transform even the most basic of rooms. Moldings embellish the perimeters of rooms and the openings within them, while railings often enhance a home's core in a more concentrated, central area. Both should look organic to the structure they embellish, adding dimension and character that appear to have always been there.

Creating Decorative Bones with Moldings

Have you ever walked into a house that has tiny baseboards, no crown moldings, and very small, flat, inexpensive-looking window and door casings? How does that home feel? Does it look substantial? Well built? I have seen many spec or tract homes that fit this description, and the answer is always a resounding "No!" Simply put, moldings can make or break a room or, for that matter, an entire home.

Of course, extremely contemporary architecture, such as that seen in many of today's lofts, is an exception here. These rooms often don't have moldings at all. The same applies to rustic

A newly remodeled Victorian retains its heritage with ornate crown molding, window casings, and baseboards. This architectural detail was carried through at the top of the new bookcase cabinets that were added on both sides of the fireplace.

architecture, which features plastered or stuccoed walls with bullnosed corners bordering windows, doors, and passageways. These, too, are devoid of moldings, and the absence of this ornamentation is appropriate for these types of architecture.

But in the more traditional styles that comprise the majority of homes across America, moldings are essential. I'm not talking about diminutive moldings or varieties that change in size and shape from room to room, but substantial, consistent moldings that edge floors, ceilings, windows, doors, and passageways throughout a home.

The style of a home should flow from room to room, and consistently sized and shaped moldings are a key factor in creating this flow. Moldings—or trim, as it is typically referred to—should all be painted or stained the same color no matter what color each room is painted, as moldings provide a common element that ties a home together. Of course, there are always exceptions. For instance, a living room with a pitched ceiling probably won't have a crown molding, while the rest of the rooms might. In this case, the baseboards and window and door trim should be treated consistently throughout the structure.

GENERAL MOLDING DEFINITIONS

Molding—A shaped decorative strip of material used to finish a surface.

Crown Molding—A molding where the wall and ceiling meet or the uppermost molding along furniture or cabinetry.

Dentil Molding—A series of small, square blocks uniformly spaced and projecting like teeth.

Baseboard—The finish trim where the floor and wall meet.

Trim—The visible woodwork or moldings of a room, such as baseboards, casings, and so on.

Casing—The exposed trim bordering, framing, or lining a door or window.

Chair Rail—A wooden molding placed along the lower part of the wall, historically used to prevent chairs from damaging the wall but now used as decoration.

Profile—A side view or view in contour.

MDF (Medium Density Fiberboard)—Wood scraps and plant fibers compressed together with a binding material such as glue and pressed out to form a sheet material, which is used in construction.

Although simple and unpretentious, these door and crown moldings once disappeared within white walls in this eclectically styled home. Now richly colored terra-cotta walls provide a strong contrast to enhance even these understated moldings, bringing definition to the room's doorway and ceiling height.

Choosing Your Moldings

Never try to pick moldings from a catalog. Unless you work in the construction trade, it is difficult to select a molding profile from a photo or drawing. Go to a lumberyard and find where the molding samples are displayed. Select several profiles in a variety of shapes and sizes and ask for at least a 12-inch sample of each. They are usually provided free of charge. Go home and tack up your samples. Always look at them from across a room. Is the size right? Are they too big for the height of the room or too small to look substantial? Are they excessively ornate or too simple for your architecture? For example, if you live in a small rustic cottage, or you want to achieve this look, you should keep the moldings simple

ABOVE: The technique used to create the detail on this plaster molding is called wall flowering. Artist Zdravko Terziev squeezes plaster from a pastry bag to create the borders and floral design that we selected to complement the Corinthian capital below.

LEFT: Plaster molding creates a feeling of elegance and formality in this Mediterranean-style dining room. The soft apricot-toned plaster molding bordering the ceiling contrasts with the golden walls, yet harmonizes in color with the mahogany wood moldings framing the windows.

and uncomplicated like the cottage itself. But if you live in a historic Victorian or Colonial home, the moldings should be elaborate. Again, always respect the architecture of your home. If you are in the process of making a new architectural statement, think about the feeling you want your home to evoke—simple yet elegant, formal yet unpretentious, or ornate and over the top—and let that feeling be your guide. Remember, we're not just interested in the way a home looks but in the way it *feels*.

ABOVE: This opening between living room and kitchen becomes statelier with the simple addition of a piece of 1 x 8-inch stock lumber to the top of the existing door molding. A 4-inch crown molding was added to the 1 x 8, raising the look of the opening by almost 11 inches.

LEFT: Crisp white moldings contrast with colorful walls that accentuate the passageways in this lively and eclectic home.

No matter how simple or ornate the moldings, always go for substantial ones and apply them consistently throughout your home. I like to use a minimum of 3- to 4-inch-wide casings, at least 3 $\frac{1}{2}$-inch crown moldings, and 5-inch baseboards or taller, depending on ceiling height. Moldings can also be layered to achieve a wider variation of door and window casings or stacked to embellish crowns and baseboards. Remember, good design repeats itself, so the crown, baseboard, and window and door moldings should all harmonize but not necessarily match. Ideally, door casings should be slightly thicker in depth than the baseboards, so the vertical trim piece stands proud of (extends beyond) the baseboard.

When building a new home or doing an extensive remodel, it is important to choose your moldings as early as possible or at least discuss the dimensions of your window and door trim with your architect, designer, or contractor before framing begins. This way, he or she can allow for the correct width of the vertical molding in relation to the floor plan.

When remodeling, if you are happy with your existing moldings and they complement the architecture and convey the feeling you want, match the size and shape or profile of what exists. If you can't find an exact match, you can have them milled by a lumberyard, specialty molding store, or specialty cabinetmaker. This can be expensive. If you can't afford custom-milled molding, pick something that is as similar as possible to your original molding in size and shape and try to avoid awkward transitions.

Moldings come in a diverse array of materials—stone, concrete, wood, plaster, metal, foam, plastic, or other synthetic materials—the latter three of which I never use. It is much better to use natural materials when at all possible.

ABOVE: Architect Dick Hunt, of Hunt Hale Jones Architects in San Francisco, combines large-scale pilasters and pediments to frame openings, giving walls, windows, and doorways size and substance. These traditional moldings make a somewhat serious and formal statement that both complements and contrasts with the colorful, playful atmosphere created in the interior of this contemporary, country guest house.

LEFT: Adding architectural detail to the passageway between living room and library in this luxurious home brings a balancing level of sophistication. To create the effect, elaborate moldings wrap the opening to make walls appear thick and a 1 x 15-inch pediment embellishes the passageway. The smooth, white-painted opening now appears wider, higher, and grander and is accentuated by softly textured butter-colored plaster walls.

Stone or concrete moldings are usually the most expensive and can be purchased at tile and stone stores or through companies that specialize in these products. They are available in a limited number of shapes and sizes but often come in a variety of colors and textures. Always get samples of the varying colors, profiles, and sizes to try on site.

Wood moldings are much less expensive and come in hundreds of different sizes and profiles. Interior moldings usually come in oak, pine, primed pine, poplar, redwood, and MDF (see sidebar on page 91). Exterior moldings can typically be purchased in fir, cedar, or redwood. Decorative treatments for wood moldings range from staining and clear coating to painting and faux painting.

Moldings can create dramatic decorative effects in homes, particularly if they are painted in a contrasting color and sheen to the walls. I love to paint walls rich and vibrant colors and then use contrasting white,

RIGHT: Pediment power indeed! Guests are welcomed at the front door, complete with wrought-iron inset and an antique metal architectural element that hangs above it, making a creatively enticing entrance.

BELOW, RIGHT: Pediments don't have to match door moldings. This small doorway had no presence or importance until we added a pediment made of knotty pine and small crown molding. The new ornament was faux painted by Arno Cornillion to give it an aged patina, harmonizing with the 100-year-old rustic cottage it complements. The broken pediment mirrors the lines of the pitched ceiling above it, helping to bring the low door and elevated room height together.

FACING PAGE: Stately columns supporting a substantial pediment span this stairwell entry hall, providing drama and strong architectural bones. We replaced the original plasterboard half-wall on this landing with a traditional wooden stairway railing that complements the architectural character of the columns and pediment.

cream, or a color slightly lighter than the walls for the moldings. As for the sheen, walls are typically painted flat with moldings covered in an eggshell, satin, or even semigloss finish. The higher the sheen, the more light that is reflected, so you may consider semigloss if the room has low light or if you really want the moldings to pop. Higher sheen paint is also easier to clean. However, the higher the sheen of a painted surface, the more imperfections are revealed, so you might not want to paint old, funky moldings in a semigloss.

Moldings that Strengthen Walls

By now, you have heard me talk a lot about fat walls and what they do for a home. Moldings are a brilliant way to create the feeling of fat walls without double framing. A typical wall, as we discussed in chapter three (Fat Arches and Deep Niches), is framed at 4 inches thick. To make the end or cross-section of a wall appear fat in a passageway without double framing the wall, simply build up the end of a wall with stock lumber layered with moldings. For example, you can add a 1 x 6-inch piece of stock lumber to both sides of the walls bordering a passageway. Layer on a piece of $^3/_4$ x 6-inch molding over the stock lumber, again on both sides of the wall. Then cover the end or cross-section with a piece of stock lumber cut to 6 $^1/_2$ inches, and you have inexpensively fattened the walls in your passageway by 3 inches. The end piece of lumber is slightly inset from both moldings but should conceal the joints.

Raising the Eye with Pediments

Just as moldings can magically make walls appear thicker, pediments can make passageways appear higher and more substantial. It's easy to create a pediment over an opening by installing a 1 x 4-, 1 x 6-, 1 x 8-, or even 1 x 12-inch piece of stock lumber in the appropriate length. Then, add a piece of crown molding on top that complements

The newel posts on this traditional stairway complement the pilasters and pediment defining the adjacent passageway. A plasterboard half-wall was replaced by a wooden railing on the landing, which harmonizes with the architecture and allows light to pass through from the window above.

the other moldings in the room. The depth of the pediment should be slightly thicker, so the vertical moldings framing the passageway can die into it when they intersect at the top of the opening. This embellishment has a strong impact if you have low openings and high ceilings. However, even a 7-foot-high opening in a 9-foot-high room can be transformed by installing a 12- to 18-inch-high pediment. Mock it up and make sure it harmonizes with the scale of the room so that it looks organic to the structure. Be sure to repeat this treatment throughout your home in other major passageways and even over windows and doors.

Pediments can be created in hundreds of combinations of shapes, sizes, moldings, and detail. They raise the eye, add architectural detail, and define passageways. These inexpensive architectural bones also add height, character, and elegance. Start noticing pediments wherever you go. They are everywhere, particularly on the exterior of buildings. Take pictures of them to get ideas. Get samples of wood and moldings to play with and mock up different sizes and configurations of pediments until you find the right combination for your rooms.

Pediments and Pilasters Combine

Moldings and stock lumber can be combined to create pilasters, which project from the walls bordering a passageway. These strong, vertical bones, as discussed in the last chapter, combine handsomely with pediments to create even more substantial and dramatic openings between rooms. Again, this combination is relatively easy to build and install and provides a big bang for your buck. Pilasters and pediments can frame openings either ornately or in an understated way, but no matter what the style, the result is a room with substantial architectural details. Whether you use moldings, pilasters, or pediments, or a combination of all three, these strong bones can border, crown, and conquer even the most insignificant and uninspired passageways. They can be added quickly and inexpensively to your home to embellish your rooms and the connections between them. And remember, when using these powerhouses, always respect your existing architecture; make sure they are designed to look original or complement the structure.

Diverse Railings

Like moldings, stairway railings offer a great opportunity to make a strong architectural statement. I like to think of stairways as the spine of a structure. If a home has wood moldings and the stairway railings are also wood, the moldings and railings should harmonize, incorporating the same shapes and design.

However, many homes today have drywall railings. These are really only appropriate in a contemporary setting, but due to construction costs, many builders, developers, and homeowners are using them regardless of the style of architecture.

If you have the choice and your home is not contemporary in style, I urge you to install an attractive open railing that complements the style of your home. A stairway is a vital architectural element, making a design statement on each level to

LEFT: In this contemporary home, a drywall stair rail gets a twist where the stairway curves to complement a rounded soffit in the adjacent ceiling. The salmon-colored stair rail interior gives an additional lift.

FACING PAGE: A solid stair rail, made of smoked glass and plate metal, was replaced with a light and airy zigzag stair rail that was ordered from a catalog, assembled, and then installed in this contemporary home.

LIKE MOLDINGS, STAIRWAY RAILINGS OFFER A GREAT OPPORTUNITY TO MAKE A STRONG ARCHITECTURAL STATEMENT.

which it provides access. An open railing—one created with individual balusters—is much less dense and heavy than a drywall railing, allowing light to pass through at every angle and turn. Stairway railings can be made of wood, stone, metal, glass, drywall, or a combination of these materials. They can be as diverse in style as homes are diverse in architecture.

Next to drywall, wood railings are the least expensive and lend themselves to a variety of designs. In addition to the style of the balustrade and newel posts, enhancing wood railings with paint can create a range of options for embellishment and definition.

Wood, metal, and stone railings can all be purchased from catalogs where individual pieces such as handrails, balusters, newel posts, and finials can be ordered, assembled by a professional, and then installed on site.

This old stairway was given a face-lift by removing carpet on the treads, refinishing the aged fir floors beneath, and then painting the handrail and stair carriage bronze to contrast with the creamy white balusters.

Wood and metal stair-rail parts ordered from catalogs can be relatively inexpensive, with stone parts being the most costly. Custom-made stair-rail elements are much more expensive, whether made in wood, metal, or stone.

When selecting a design for a new stair rail, try to repeat or harmonize with other elements in the structure. Find pictures of interesting stair rails; there are many diverse styles. Talk to your contractor about reproducing a design you like. Look through railing catalogs, order samples of different elements, and then have your contractor or ironworker mock up a section for your approval. Create a railing with strength, structure, and character that reflects the feeling of your architecture and commands presence as a central focus in your home's interior.

LEFT: Multiple materials were combined to create this dramatic stairway in a Wine Country estate. A handmade, 12-inch-diameter newel post embellished with composite leaves anchors the stair rail made of custom-designed iron balusters.

FACING PAGE: We opened and expanded the once-boxed-in entry to this elegant Mediterranean home by replacing a heavy half-wall with a more delicate wrought-iron railing. The curve of the railing mimics the ceiling above the entry and complements the arched front door.

Imaginative CABINETRY

"The home should be the treasure chest of living."

—LE CORBUSIER

THE CABINETS IN OUR HOMES, which hold many of our treasures and present large palettes to work with, can provide rooms with really good bones or building blocks for design. Cabinets should look organic to a structure and relate to the architectural style, but, in addition, cabinets should enhance a home, creating beauty as well as function. Considering the price of cabinets today, and the number of years you're going to live with them, it is well worth investing some time and energy into making these treasure chests beautiful and, for that matter, unusual.

Cabinets don't have to take the same old traditional shape we tend to think cabinets should. They don't always need to have doors, or their doors can hide things we might not typically think of hiding, such as entire home offices! Cabinets can be embellished in countless ways. And for those existing cabinets that are looking worn around the edges, dated, or a little too slick, there are some rehab techniques that don't cost an arm and a leg. So open up your mind and your imagination—and maybe even your cabinets—and think outside the box. Consider creating treasure chests to hold the favorite things you use every day to make your life function.

FACING PAGE: The style and embellishment of these French country cabinets set this room apart. We furnished this kitchen rather than filling it with matching boxes. The glazed maple pantry on the left boasts an arched bonnet top and oak appliqué, while the black island topped with antiqued onyx is enhanced with composite corbels.

Choosing New Cabinets and Doors

If you're considering new cabinets in your home, what can you do that's different? Consider designing cabinets that look like furniture. Give them feet, arched bonnets, bead-board backing, or interesting hardware with exposed hinges. Think about *furnishing* your kitchen or bathroom, not just installing matching cabinets everywhere. Just as you wouldn't buy every piece of furniture in the same color or fabric, don't make all your kitchen or bathroom elements the same. Give them several designs and finishes, use different materials, pick varying door styles, or add different moldings or appliqués.

Whenever possible take cabinets to the ceiling—not just in kitchens and bathrooms but wherever you can. Gone are the days of leaving space above cabinets to collect dust, look barren, or fill with plastic plants. Tall cabinets can make a room look bigger and grander, whereas low cabinets stop the eye and diminish a room. I do make an exception for rooms that have over 9-foot-high ceilings.

If your new cabinets have doors, picking a door style is an important factor in creating the look you want. There are many companies that exclusively sell cabinet doors in a wide variety of materials and styles. In addition, you can give old cabinets a new look simply by replacing the doors. Just bear in mind that this works best with painted cabinetry, as matching stain-grade woods can be difficult.

Cabinets with flat doors—without paneling or molding—look very contemporary and are generally the least expensive, depending on the material used. Recessed panel doors without moldings can also look contemporary or

ABOVE: We created an eight-section cubby cabinet to extend the small kitchen counter in this colorful guest house. The cabinet positions dishware and glasses within comfortable reach. In addition, the 10-inch-deep, bead-board-backed cabinet serves as a divider between the kitchen and small office/bedroom above.

LEFT: This bathroom was transformed by the unusual 8-foot-high corner cabinet that we designed and had custom made for the tiny space by artist John Hull. The high-gloss black cabinet with red interior presents items for easy access, takes very little floor space, contains two electrical outlets, and includes a closed compartment for tucking away special items. By thinking outside the box, sorely needed utility arrived dramatically dressed.

can create a Shaker or Arts & Crafts look. Recessed panel doors with thick or heavy moldings look more traditional or rustic and are often used in country or Mediterranean interiors. Raised panel doors, usually the highest priced, are the most elaborate and traditional in style, lending themselves to more formal or ornate homes.

In addition to picking a door style, you'll need to choose either a paint-grade or stain-grade material. Paint-grade doors are usually made out of poplar, alder, or MDF and are cheaper to purchase, yet require

professional finishing in order to look good and wear well. These doors can be painted, glazed, or faux finished. Stain-grade doors come in maple, red and white oak, pine (with or without knots), cherry, walnut, beech, mahogany, ash, fir, redwood, and alder or can be custom ordered in almost any species of exotic wood you can imagine. Rare woods are, of course, the most expensive; maple is usually one of the least expensive cabinet materials.

Stain-grade doors or cabinets can be clear coated or stained to deepen or enrich the color.

Cabinets without doors are sometimes a good choice, particularly in small rooms. They often make a room look larger, providing perspective for the eye. They offer not only an opportunity to embellish the interior of the cabinet to contrast with the face frame but also a venue in which to display your treasures and give you unimpeded access to the contents. On the downside, open cabinets can look bad if you are totally disorganized and messy. Some household items are meant to be hidden. If you don't feel comfortable about completely eliminating cabinet doors, you may want to select doors that have glass or wire inset panels. Clear or opaque glass panels are available in many different designs and textures. The wire insets range from rustic-looking chicken wire to more contemporary wire designs. Shop the internet or ask your contractor for sources. These options can soften or disguise what's inside your cabinets, while providing visual interest from the outside.

General Cabinet Terms

Face frame–style cabinet—Cabinets that have a hardwood frame on the face of the cabinet box that masks the raw edges of the plywood or particleboard sides, adds rigidity to the cabinet, and provides a strong base for attaching hinges.

Frameless- or European-style cabinet—A cabinet that replaces the solid wood face frame with edge banding, usually offering no reveal of the box itself, creating a more contemporary look. Hinges attach to doors and side or end panels of the box and are typically concealed.

Rail—A horizontal member of a panel or frame.

Stile—A vertical member of a panel or frame.

Recessed panel door—A flat or grooved panel set within the frame of a door.

Raised panel door—A door panel that has been routed, shaped, or otherwise decorated to have a higher profile than a flat panel.

European hinge—Fully concealed hinge that is mortised into the inside of the cabinet frame or door and is often adjustable.

Butt hinge—An exposed hinge composed of two plates attached to abutting surfaces of a door and doorjamb and joined by a pin.

Appliqué—A carved or otherwise decorative piece of material applied to the surface of another material.

Country juxtaposes with contemporary in this whimsical kitchen, where simple maple combines with rustic bead board for an unexpected cabinet combo. Above a collection of handmade pottery, four puck lights on a dimmer create a glow in the country cupboard that is embellished with aged and distressed ornate moldings. Playful, decorative hardware completes the connection of the eclectic elements.

Artist John Hull constructed this red aniline-dyed contemporary maple bookcase as a brilliant receptacle for the owners' treasured book collection. We designed the floor-to-ceiling grid to reflect the lines of the surrounding cityscape, giving the bookcase backdrop a strong aesthetic statement.

Creative Cabinet Embellishment

While you're thinking outside the box—which, by the way, should be a permanent state of mind when creating rooms with good bones—think embellishment. How can you embellish your cabinets in ways that might be new and innovative? Here are a few ideas.

The simplest way to transform cabinets is to paint them. The color and sheen you choose depends on the feeling you're trying to create—simple and serene, funky and fun, brilliant and outrageous, or formal and elegant. Always consider the light in the room where you plan to paint, as well as the size of the room. If it's a small, dark, enclosed room consider keeping walls and cabinets the same color and the sheen higher to reflect light. If your room is large or open and bright, you have more options for using contrasting wall and cabinet colors or finishes. Sometimes, just painting the walls a bright color in contrast to the cabinets can be transformational (see photo on page 116/117). Cabinets are easier to clean if they are painted at least in a satin finish, which I find most people choose. If you're using a semigloss paint, be sure your cabinets are in good shape, as the higher sheen will reveal any imperfections in the material.

When selecting colors for your cabinets, also consider the color of your floors, tile, or counters—anything that won't change in the room. Rooms should flow from one to another, so using the same colors in different values or tones as you have in other parts of your home is often a good choice.

Just about anything can be painted, including laminate or cabinets that have been lacquered. It's all a matter of prep and durability. I recommend taking a cabinet door to your local paint store for suggestions on prep and products or to discuss the correct procedure for your cabinets with your painter.

ALWAYS CONSIDER THE LIGHT IN THE ROOM WHERE YOU PLAN TO PAINT, AS WELL AS THE SIZE OF THE ROOM.

To create a space for a funky table for two, the upper cabinets in this kitchen were extended beyond the lowers, providing the perfect place for an old Mexican table to reside. The open shelves give depth to the small kitchen and provide display space for a colorful handmade pottery and glass collection.

Always try paint samples wherever you decide to paint. You can sample right on your cabinet, but it's preferable to paint a piece of poster board and put it up with construction tape on your cabinets. Try it in different parts of the room. Look at it with lights on, lights off, in the morning, at noon, and at night. Always look at color samples from across the room.

Distressing, antiquing, glazing, and faux painting cabinets can create an endless variety of looks. Also, a finish technique where cabinets are aniline dyed (applied with a transparent stain in a color such as red, green, or yellow) can be quite dramatic and unusual. This is typically done in more contemporary projects and on wood with a strong grain.

A dated wine cabinet, once covered with a heavy oak door, becomes an enticing bar area complete with shelving for glassware and a marble slab for serving drinks. The open cabinet, which perceptively adds space to the small *pied à terre*, is lit from within by recessed cans and from without by ceiling lights.

I design a lot of cabinetry with distressing and antiquing, as they are easy to live with. If a child or pet gouges a cabinet or scratches the finish, it rarely shows when the surface has been aged. Find a good decorative painter who can show you his or her portfolio. Ask to look at samples of the painter's work for ideas on what type of finish you want. There are many to choose from. Again, go with the feeling you are trying to create. Don't be afraid to take a risk, do something different, and be creative.

This small contemporary kitchen installed in a converted French laundry looked gray and forlorn until we painted the walls a bright persimmon. The vivid paint transformed the space, making the dull laminate cabinets with black counters and backsplash come to life.

I think of hardware as the jewelry on a cabinet. Adding or changing hardware is a high-impact way to transform cabinets. Just add some decorative hardware and you create a whole new feeling. But hardware, like jewelry, can look cheap and if it does, it will detract from the look and feel of your room. Pick the best quality hardware you can afford. Be sure to measure the length and width of your cabinet's stiles to make sure the hardware will fit. Hardware comes in thousands of styles, sizes, and finishes. Always go with the feeling you're trying to create—elegant, rustic, traditional, or contemporary, for example. Pick a finish that goes well with all the elements in your room—paint, tile, countertops. You should try to harmonize your cabinet hardware with door hardware and plumbing fixtures in the room, but they don't need to match.

So many homes I've visited have cabinets without any hardware at all. Adding decorative hardware can truly transform potentially handsome bones. Moldings can also change a mundane cabinet into a magnificent one. I've often just added some big, beefy crown molding to the top of kitchen or bathroom cabinets and the whole room takes on a new look. Adding molding or even pediments to cabinets can close those unsightly gaps between cabinet and ceiling and take even the plainest cabinets from uninspired to imaginative.

Appliqués are another great way to embellish cabinets. They come in wood or composite, are easy to apply, and can add interest and dimension to your cabinets. There are several companies that make

Cabinet Rehab 101. (1) Take a small, dated kitchen and replace the upper cabinet door panels with glass to give depth and a feeling of space; (2) paint the inside of the uppers to harmonize with the brick wall; (3) paint the upper and lower cabinets a soft, glossy gray to blend with the stainless steel appliances; (4) add interesting hardware; (5) light the upper cabinets with track lighting; and (6) transformation! For before and after photos, see the Finale on page 148.

appliqués (see the resource list on page 155). The wood variety is the most expensive. Composite appliqués are available in countless assortments and can be inexpensive. Wood appliqués can be stained or painted; composite varieties must always be painted. These elements add detailed ornamentation to your cabinetry, giving it a hand-carved look if applied and finished properly.

I always try to accent interesting cabinetry with lighting, usually track or recessed cans that can be projected onto the face of the cabinets. Lighting possibilities expand when you have cabinets with glass doors or no doors at all. These open cabinets give you the opportunity to light the interiors, perhaps reflecting off a contrasting color. If you have glass shelves, small puck lights can be added at the top of the

LEFT: We selected composite scroll-shaped appliqués to adorn this European country–bathroom cabinet. The dentil molding below each set of scrolls is bordered by a pair of pilasters that extends from the tiled floor to support a limestone-slab counter detail. The arched mirror molding repeats the dentil detail.

BELOW: Our goal was to furnish this French country kitchen, not fill it with matching cabinetry. The island and cabinets that border the hood are clear-coated fir, all lower perimeter cabinets are faux painted gold, and the one green cabinet to the right of the sink simply stands alone.

ABOVE: The rustic, antiqued green cabinet with substantial crown and dentil molding displays colorful dishes through chicken wire insets in the arched and branded doors. A branding iron, custom made in the shape of a diamond, was heated and pressed into the painted cabinet doors, creating an unusual texture and pattern.

FACING PAGE: This imposing stained-and-sandblasted alder cabinet commands the focal point in this Wine Country kitchen. Bold crown and dentil moldings above a pediment with composite appliqués embellish this richly detailed armoire-style cabinet, which houses a refrigerator on the right and pantry on the left.

cabinet to illuminate the entire interior. If you have wooden shelves, you can run either incandescent, halogen, or low-voltage lighting horizontally under each shelf or vertically behind the face frame on either side of the opening of your cabinet. A lighting plan should be specified before ordering new cabinets so they can be made to accommodate any interior fixtures. Discuss your lighting ideas with your contractor, electrician and cabinet maker. Put cabinet lighting on a separate switch if possible and always on a dimmer. It creates a wonderful effect to have cabinet lights on in the evening in an otherwise dark kitchen.

A floor-to-ceiling Chinese-red cabinet, filled with 48 drawers, makes a powerful design statement in this contemporary multi-purpose room. Some drawers house files, paperwork, and office supplies, while others open to expose a hidden desk, computer, scanner, copier, fax, and phone. A large television sits behind four swing-open faux drawers, making this office, media, and guest room functional yet surprising with its hidden agenda.

Hidden Agendas

When planning your next cabinet purchase, think about what, if anything, you might want to hide or even disguise. It may be your blender or coffeemaker in an appliance garage or your refrigerator in what looks to be an armoire. It could be your TV—flat screens included—or your computer, fax, copier, and scanner. It could even be your entire desk. If there's anything in your home that you hate looking at every day, consider a cabinet cover up. They can hide what's unattractive and create beauty at the same time.

Cabinets are important, functional elements in your home that you use every day. Whether you are buying new cabinets or rehabbing old ones, use your imagination and think creatively.

Go to a kitchen-and-bath showroom and check out the cabinet styles and finishes. Look at hardware over the internet or at your local hardware store. Get molding samples and mock them up on top of your cabinets, or try adding detail to plain door fronts. Order appliqué catalogs,

This French country–kitchen cabinetry emulates furniture with its different door styles, hardware, and finishes. The glazed maple pantry on the right sports tall handles with rustic backplates and butt hinges. The faux painted terra-cotta-colored cabinet is embellished with larger, recessed panels and a different style of hardware in the same finish. This richly colored cabinet hides two 27-inch Sub Zero units—a refrigerator on the right and freezer on the left.

select a few designs, and get samples. Play with lighting and paint. Order cabinets in unusual shapes, or put them in unusual places. Choose carefully what to display and what to hide. Break a few rules (but always respect your architecture!). And whatever you do, don't take cabinets for granted. There's simply no reason to compromise these important bones by allowing them to be boring and lackluster. Let your imagination lead the way, and don't be boxed in. When it comes to cabinets, the box is only the beginning.

FIREPLACE
Focal Points

FACING PAGE: Designed to complement the architecture of this new home, this dramatic fireplace features a heavily plastered overmantel, angled to pull the eye up to the room's vaulted ceiling. The antique metal surround enhances the design with a curve that softens the opening and adds contrasting texture and color. Although this living room is relatively small, the commanding fireplace creates a feeling of grandeur.

FIREPLACES ARE ONE OF THE MOST IMPORTANT BONES in a structure. Often located in the center of a home, fireplaces beckon us, providing a place of warmth, beauty, enticing sounds, and wonderful smells. A fireplace is not only an area of gathering but also an important visual focal point.

In today's architecture, however, fireplaces are not always treated as they historically were. They don't have the presence or attention to detail they once had. They are often made of drywall or slabs of slick granite pieced together around an unattractive black box. Because of the cost and sometimes the code restrictions on building masonry fireplaces, we're seeing more inexpensive, zero-clearance wood- and gas-burning inserts, which can be stark, sterile, and unattractive. Mantels are often prefabricated, and the glass doors that once opened to connect you to the fire have given way to solid glass walls, which make the gas fire behind them look surreal and disconnected. In many new homes, instead of building a fire with wood and kindling, you simply flip a switch.

I like old-fashioned fireplaces that I can hear, smell, and feel. Yes, there are code restrictions today that limit the types of new fireplaces you can build, but whenever possible, make your fireplace assume its natural role as a focal point that warms and

LEFT: The mantel and overmantel made of drywall and plaster are further enhanced by a concrete egg and dart molding, then topped with layers of various sized wooden crown moldings.

BELOW: Once a mere "hole in the wall" with no mantel, this fireplace is now distinctive. We designed stainless steel curves to support yet contrast with a new 6 x 6-inch distressed fir–beam mantel. The mantel surround was heavily plastered and faux painted by Arno Cornillion. The simple and silvery custom-made fireplace screen, oversized for the firebox, gives the illusion of a grander opening.

ABOVE: The Rumford fireplace opening was adjusted to accommodate this antique Victorian metal fireplace surround, which adds soul and character to the new fireplace.

comforts you. If you are remodeling or building a new home, plan a special location for a fireplace or, better yet, multiple locations for fireplaces that have character and detail. Or, if you have a dated or lackluster fireplace that doesn't provide a strong focal point, give it a face-lift. It's easier than you think.

Brand-New and Grand

Building a new fireplace is like piecing together a puzzle. The process can be delightful, but to start you need a plan of the home you are building or remodeling. Where would a fireplace fit? Where would you use it the most? What room could accommodate seating around a fireplace? How would it be vented? Could you have more than one?

Always attempt to put a fireplace in the center of a major living area in your home, but don't make the mistake of blocking a beautiful view. It's okay to have two focal points—a view and a fireplace—but some people have television screens as focal points. In my opinion, these take third place. We are seeing an unfortunate trend toward putting television screens above fireplaces. Please avoid this whenever possible. It diminishes the importance of the fireplace and detracts significantly from its beauty. Try to plan your room so that the TV can be viewed from a separate location while letting you enjoy the fire.

Now, back to your floor plan. When positioning your fireplace, it's always a good idea to include scaled drawings of furniture to make sure you have plenty of seating area around the fire. If you're not working with a floor plan, measure and tape out on the floor where you could place your furniture around the fireplace. Also, think about what you want on either side of your fireplace focal point—windows, doors, bookcases, built-ins?

To design the fireplace itself, start with the firebox. Prefabricated inserts are the least expensive option and come in a variety of sizes, as do Rumford kits. Masonry fireplaces can be built any size, depending on building codes in your area, but are by far the most expensive alternative. Your contractor can explain your options.

Select the largest firebox your space can handle, always keeping in mind the scale of your room. Once the type of firebox is selected, consider where it will be placed on the wall. Will it be at floor level, elevated

> ALWAYS ATTEMPT TO PUT A FIREPLACE IN THE CENTER OF A MAJOR LIVING AREA IN YOUR HOME, BUT DON'T MAKE THE MISTAKE OF BLOCKING A BEAUTIFUL VIEW.

Intricately molded concrete tiles are installed floor to ceiling, giving this elevated gas-burning firebox presence and, with a heavy grout slurry, substance. The fireplace surround is further embellished with a concrete lintel below and two concrete corbels topped with a mahogany mantel that gives depth and perspective to the flat fireplace. The handmade screen opens for access to the fire and covers the unattractive border of the metal firebox insert.

above the floor to allow for a raised hearth, or even higher on the wall to permit viewing from a bed or perhaps another room? Be aware that a highly elevated fireplace can end up looking like a bread oven or a floating box. For this reason, whenever possible, design a raised hearth under an elevated fireplace. This tends to ground it and make it look more authentic. However, if this is not possible given the height of the opening and the amount of floor space available, you can try adding details that create depth and perspective.

Once the size and height of the firebox are determined, decide whether you need a fireplace surround. If your mantel is made of rock, stone, concrete, metal, drywall, or plaster, it is noncombustible. This means your mantel can border your firebox without an alternate fireplace surround. With a wooden mantel, you must allow for a surround of noncombustible material in between the firebox and the mantel or mantelpiece. Your local building code will dictate the minimum size the surround needs to be.

The hearth is often made of the same material as the surround, and its dimension must also meet code requirements. The decision to have a raised or flat hearth usually depends on the size of your room and your furniture placement. Do you have enough space for a raised hearth? Will your furniture placement accommodate it? I like designing fireplaces with raised hearths; they are wonderful places to sit and warm yourself by the fire and they also provide extra seating for large gatherings. However, you may want

This romantic guesthouse with lofty 13-foot ceilings was built with a small firebox installed at floor level. To bring the scale of the fireplace into a more pleasing proportion with the room, we added a drywall surround and overmantel in the shape of a fireplace with angled shoulders and a chimney top. Two antique metal corbels give dimension and solidity, while a large dentil molding topped by a second crown molding adds detail. A 4 x 8-inch aged-and-distressed plank completes the mantel, and an overscaled, rustic, metal fireplace screen made by Brian Kennedy covers the unattractive firebox.

A simple mantel found at an antique store gives the '50s-era tract home soul and character and transforms the once white-brick fireplace into a unique focal point.

a more European or even contemporary look, in which a fireplace sits at floor level. The size or layout of your room will often determine whether you use a raised hearth or one at floor level.

In determining the size and look of a wooden mantel or mantelpiece once the firebox, surround, and hearth have been chosen, first decide if the structure will simply sit above the fireplace opening or will have vertical components on each side. A mantelpiece, which sits above the firebox, should extend beyond the opening on each side. How far it should extend should be based on the size of the opening, the wall the fireplace is placed on, and the scale of the room. The dimensions of the mantelpiece (as well as a mantel with legs), in terms of thickness and depth of each component, should be based on the same considerations as mentioned above. I prefer to install substantial mantels and mantelpieces that command a strong focal point in a room. The style of the mantel or mantelpiece depends on the architecture of the room and the feeling you are trying to project—be it contemporary, traditional, rustic, Southwestern or old-world.

There are many companies that make prefabricated stone, concrete, and wood mantels that are attractive—ask your contractor for catalogs. You can also go to salvage yards or antique stores and find wonderful old fireplace mantels and surrounds that can be incorporated into your design, or you can have a mantel built. There are quite a few books available on fireplaces in which you can research ideas. Find a picture of a fireplace you like and ask your contractor to duplicate it, ideally adding some personal touches to make it your own.

GENERAL FIREPLACE DEFINITIONS

Firebox—The chamber of a fireplace in which fuel is burned.

Hearth—An area of noncombustible material that the firebox sits on. It can be raised or at floor level.

Surround—The noncombustible material usually on all three sides of a fireplace opening.

Mantel—The construction or facing around a fireplace.

Mantelpiece—The fittings and decorative elements of a mantel above a fireplace.

Overmantel—A decorative structure or ornamental panel above a mantelpiece or mantel.

Rumford fireplace—A fireplace that is tall and shallow to reflect more heat, with a streamlined throat to eliminate turbulence and carry away the smoke with little loss of heated room air.

Zero-clearance fireplace gas or wood inserts—A fireplace that can be installed with wooden framing directly against the metal stand-offs on the fireplace's openings.

Masonry fireplace—A fireplace made of stone, rock, or brick.

ABOVE: This antique mantel, which covers a dated white-brick fireplace, is embellished with a rusted architectural element, placed for additional depth and texture.

RIGHT: This new fireplace, added during a remodel to update a Victorian home, started as a small metal firebox with a white marble surround and white wooden mantel. Only the size and shape of the mantel were right for the architecture of the room. The transformation required two simple steps—painting the mantel high-gloss black and thin-setting colorful handmade tiles in the room's palette directly on the marble surround.

FACING PAGE: The original but uninspired white-marble fireplace was faux painted to look like old stone and then topped by a painted wooden mantel that was designed to give some curved perspective to this living room focal point.

LEFT: We enhanced this fireplace with a white-painted mantel and black granite surround simply by painting the formerly white walls a lovely blue-green. The black surround makes the fireplace box appear larger than it is.

FACING PAGE: An apricot-colored overmantel extends to the sides of this bright red fireplace mantel that replaced a 2-inch-wide piece of white molding that framed the 100-year-old masonry fireplace. Red crown molding tops the overmantel, which was heavily textured to give it strength and presence, while old iron metal stars embellish the mantel.

The last piece of the puzzle in designing your fireplace might be the inclusion of an overmantel, which is installed above your mantel and can take a variety of shapes. I encourage this addition in fireplace design, particularly if there are high ceilings in a room. An overmantel can add a dramatic element that gives a fireplace strength, presence, and character. The overmantel can easily be built out of drywall, either going straight up from the ends of the mantel or forming an angled or even irregular shape at any point along the way. Overmantels can be covered with wood, rock, stone, tile, plaster, or paint. When painting an overmantel, I often like to use a contrasting color and texture from that of the wall to give it more presence, unless the room is very small and to do so would stop the eye.

CREATING A NEW FIREPLACE:

◆ Determine where in your home the fireplace will be placed, how it will be vented, and how furniture will be placed around it for seating.

◆ Will it sit between two windows, be bordered by two bookcases or built-ins, be in the center of a wall, or be in a corner between two angled walls?

◆ Select the firebox insert, size of the masonry kit, or dimensions of the masonry firebox.

◆ Determine if the mantel or mantelpiece will be wood or made of a noncombustible material.

◆ If the mantel is wooden, select a noncombustible material to install around the firebox such as tile, concrete, stone, or drywall; determine the dimensions the surround must be, based off your local building code. Determine size and noncombustible material of hearth.

◆ Based on the size of your firebox, surround or lack of surround, fireplace wall, and scale of room, select a mantel or mantelpiece that meets code requirements, that has the visual weight, style, and feeling you want, and that complements your architecture.

◆ Determine if an overmantel would be appropriate for your fireplace and establish the dimensions and shape.

◆ Determine the finish of the mantel or mantelpiece and overmantel if there is one. Remember, a good way to help you make each decision as you progress through these steps is to mock it up!

This metal contemporary fireplace is transformed with apricot and salmon paint covering its gray tubular frame, while gold leaf stripes enhance the fire's sparkle.

ABOVE: Amber-colored candles light up this fireplace, transforming an empty black hole into a series of multiple, glowing flames. We designed the fireplace screen, which was hand made by artist Dan Argraves of Iron Horse Ironworks, to repeat shapes from the mantel detail and cover the outside border of the unattractive gas-burning firebox insert.

FACING PAGE: Another rehabilitated fireplace with a simple formula. Rustic, colorful thin-set tiles on the surround team with a painted high-gloss black wood mantel, and *voilà!*—transformation from a boring, white-marbled spec-house fireplace to a dramatic and sparkling focal point.

If your home has a prefabricated firebox insert, I would suggest ultimately removing the glass doors and replacing them with a custom-made metal fireplace screen. A fireplace, whether gas or wood burning, that allows access to the fire looks so much more authentic than a glassed-in one. A fireplace screen can be designed to complement any type of décor in a room. A good metal- or ironworker can build a frame to cover the firebox onto which doors can be hinged to easily open and close when tending a fire. If you are in the process of selecting your firebox, avoid glassed-in units, but know that a hinged screen can disguise the glass covering. If you have the choice, always go for what looks authentic to a true fireplace.

Fireplace Face-Lifts

I've worked in many homes where the fireplaces were not designed to be important focal points. In order to keep costs down, builders or developers installed zero-clearance inserts with inexpensive marble or granite surrounds set within un-inspired, prefabricated wood mantels. The mantels are usually painted white to match the trim in the home. The result—a lackluster fireplace that doesn't really command attention nor have the presence needed to be a strong focal point in a room. I've also encountered many old fireplaces that were unfortunately not classically designed and now look stodgy and dated. There's hope for both the new, soulless variations and the vintage-but-dated fireplaces—a fireplace face-lift.

If your fireplace has a slab surround, it is fairly uncomplicated to thin-set tile over the existing slab. Ask your contractor or tile setter what is possible. I have had handmade tile installed over boring marble slab surrounds, leaving the marble hearth in the floor as it is. Of course, you can also tile the hearth, but this might not be necessary if the slab is fairly simple and you choose a tile that works with the marble. Once the tile is thin-set in place, try painting the wood mantel a dramatic color. You now have a new focal point, with rich color and texture and without a lot of cost.

Dated tile or unattractive marble or granite can also be painted for a fresh, new look. Talk to a skilled faux painter about what is possible to change the look of your tile or stone fireplace surround. With dated-looking rock fireplaces, I have enlisted a faux

A brick hearth and fireplace surround are painted high-gloss black to reflect the firelight from this masonry fireplace. The simple mantel, originally painted white, takes on a more substantial sophistication in bronze, while the coral-colored overmantel and golden yellow artwork, chair, and pillow enhance the fire's glow.

finisher to paint the rocks a more pleasing color, and then added a heavy grout slurry over the rocks, giving them an entirely different texture and feeling. A tile setter can also perform a grout slurry, which is basically smearing grout over the entire rock fireplace, then wiping part of it off before it dries. Ask your tile setter to see his array of grout color samples, and study them carefully before making your selection. Have him test the effect of the grout slurry in a small area, wiping it off quickly in case you decide not to slurry the entire fireplace.

TRY PAINTING YOUR MANTEL A BRILLIANT COLOR OR HIGH-GLOSS BLACK, OR CONSIDER PLASTERING YOUR OVERMANTEL WITH LOTS OF TEXTURE.

There are countless ways to transform existing mantels, as long as you always respect your architecture and the scale of the room the fireplace occupies. Try painting your mantel a brilliant color or high-gloss black, or consider plastering your overmantel with lots of texture. Replace your existing mantel with a fabulous old mantel from an antique or salvage store. Embellish your wood mantel with big, chunky moldings, or hang iron elements on it. Design an interesting fireplace screen to cover the firebox.

Whatever materials you choose, remember to light your fire. Use your fireplace as it was intended— to warm, nurture, and draw people to it. Embellish your fireplace to make it visually stronger and give it more presence. If you're building a new fireplace, make it special and unusual. Do something different— set it apart from all the others you've seen. If you can't light real fires in your fireplace, fill it with candles that you can light for a radiance that will make the room and everyone in it glow.

The gold-and-red chairs and candles contrast and complement this grand Rumford fireplace with approximately a 4 x 4-foot opening inside the massive gray concrete fireplace mantel. The overmantel is made with framing materials and drywall and then covered with heavy plaster that has been color-washed for aging and durability.

FINALE

M. A. ROSANOFF: "Mr. Edison, please tell me what laboratory rules you want me to observe."

THOMAS EDISON: "Hell! There ain't no rules around here. We're trying to accomplish somep'n!"

(LEFT) BEFORE

(FACING PAGE) AFTER: A 13-foot-long bathroom counter presented a challenge in remodeling this dark and dated master bath. The new combination of stylized cabinets provides tall vertical bones to break up the long horizontal line and creates beauty, interest, and function while bringing a furniture-like feeling to the updated bathroom.

AS YOU BEGIN TO CREATE AND WORK with rooms with good bones, keep in mind the following:

1. Always find the best team of people to work with.

2. Think outside the box and listen to your gut.

3. Respect the architecture and repeat design elements that work.

4. Spend some time researching what you like in books and magazines.

5. Look at structures wherever you go, and notice their bones or lack thereof.

6. Take photos and ask questions.

7. Keep a notebook of your ideas, sources, paint chips, and so on.

8. Explore salvage and lumberyards, kitchen-and-bath showrooms, and houses for sale in your neighborhood.

9. Observe with a critical eye what you like and don't like.

10. Make one decision at a time and go for the feeling you want to create.

11. Create bones in your home that will have staying power. Not only think about what you love but also what you'll still love and enjoy years from now, whether it's classically modern or classically traditional.

12. Don't just copy a picture out of a book—put your own spin on it.

(ABOVE) BEFORE

(LEFT) AFTER: A remodeled fireplace brought new life to this 1970s-era contemporary home. An overwhelming large and solid brick façade once rose almost to the ceiling, closing off the light (and, seemingly, breath) and dramatically dating the home. Now, a streamlined charcoal-plastered fireplace—with a notch for extra surprise—is a fabulously pleasing focal point. The smaller scale allows easy flow of both traffic and spirit between the two rooms and makes a thoroughly "today" statement in function and feeling.

Finally, they say a picture is worth a thousand words. I hope these "before" and "after" shots will inspire you to take on the challenge of adding, embellishing, or enhancing some good bones or architectural details in your home. Some of what these homeowners did cost a lot of money, some very little. But everyone had fun in the process, learned a lot, grew in new ways, and transformed their homes.

Remember, it's not just about the way a room looks but the way it *feels!* The trick is first to uncover or create the bones and then enhance and embellish them. The journey will inevitably have good days and challenging ones, but you will always be learning something new, not only about your home as you explore it, but about yourself as you uncover who you are, what you like, and ways you can express your creativity. In the end, your home will be a product of your vision, team effort, fun, and hard work—a home that is truly your own.

(RIGHT) BEFORE

(BELOW) AFTER: Transformation occurs in this newly expansive galley kitchen that underwent a simple face-lift from its former tiny, monotone, '60s self. The bordering post and beam are beefed up with additional layers of drywall and wood-tone faux painting, while dated oak plywood is replaced with bead board paneling under the bar. Glass panels are inserted in the newly painted cabinet doors to create depth, exposing brilliant color inside and creating a warm and welcome feeling along with the perception of more space.

(LEFT) BEFORE

(ABOVE) AFTER: An inexpensive fireplace makeover breathes new life into this tired *pied à terre* that feels stuck in time. Painting the brick fireplace surround black expands the look of the opening, while the new bronze-colored mantel adds strength and presence. The salmon-colored overmantel provides a defining vertical line, which visually raises the ceiling and warms the feeling in the room.

Finale 149

(Right) Before

(Below) After: A slightly pitched ceiling embellished with decorative beams adds a classic old-world feeling to this vintage Mediterranean home. Newly remodeled, the warm plaster walls, rich mahogany windows, and honed gold-and-terra-cotta tile and stone update the look of the dark and shiny tub deck and art deco windows installed during a 1980s remodel.

(LEFT) BEFORE

(ABOVE) AFTER: Having been stripped of its character and looking inexpensively built, this once-majestic 1920s Mediterranean home had lost all its soul through multiple remodels. After we replaced the thin wall with grand old Ionic columns, added elegant new windows, and installed beautiful moldings and window casings, the renewed structure now soulfully reflects the feeling of its original architecture.

(ABOVE) BEFORE

(RIGHT) AFTER: The living room of this traditional home visually expands in size with a new fireplace design that replaces the original small mantel with a mirror above. The new mantel and overmantel, both made of stained concrete tiles, create a commanding focal point with a feeling of timeless character and classic appeal.

Remember, there are no rules when it comes to enhancing your home's architectural character, but there are principles. Many of those principles have been covered in this book, and they will help you through the design process. Don't forget to think outside the box, give your rooms some good bones, and create the home you love. Something magical just might happen along the way.

PHOTOGRAPHY CREDITS

Russell Abraham
309 4th St. #108
Oakland, CA 94607
Phone 510-444-5204 1-2, 1-16
www.rabrahamphoto.com
pages 19 and 38

Grey Crawford
820 Bishops Lodge Road
Santa Fe, NM 87501
Phone 213-220-8968 1-12
www.greycrawford@comcast.net
pages 28 (bottom), 44 (bottom), and 79

Ken Gutmaker
5 Winfield Street
San Francisco, CA 94110
Phone 415-305-6050
www.kengutmaker.com
pages 9, 26, 27, 43, 60, 64, 65, 75, 119
(bottom), 125, and 126 (top)

David Duncan Livingston
1036 Erica Road
Mill Valley, CA 94941
Phone 415-383-0898
www.davidduncanlivingston.com
pages 10, 97, 115, 126 (bottom, right), and
131

Allen V. Lott
P.O. Box 571
Novato, CA 94947
Phone 415-897-0899
pages 28 (top), 114, and 118

Douglas A. Salin
647 Joost Avenue
San Francisco, CA 94127
Phone 415-584-3322
www.dougsalin.com
page 42

Claudio Santini
12915 Greene Avenue
Los Angeles, CA 90066
Phone 310-578-7919
www.claudiosantini.com
all others

Baan Lae Suan Magazine
Mr. Jirasak Thongyuak
Mr. Rithirong Chanthongsuk
Amarin Printing and Publishing
65/101-3 Chaiyapruk Road, Talingchan,
Bangkok 10170 THAILAND
Tel: 66 2 422 9999 Ext 4200
pages 7 and 129

SOURCES

The following is a list of vendors and sources for building or remodeling your home.

Appliances

Sub-Zero Freezer Company
P.O. Box 44130
Madison, WI 53711
800-222-7820
608-270-3339 (fax)
szmktg@subzero.com
www.subzero.com

Standards of Excellence
(Formerly McPhails)
530 West Francisco Boulevard
San Rafael, CA 94901
415-453-6070
415-453-8234 (fax)
www.standardsofexcellence.com

Cherin's
727 Valencia Street
San Francisco, CA 94110
415-864-2111
415-864-0610 (fax)
cherins@pacbell.net
www.cherins.homeappliances.com

Architects

Hank Bruce Architects
23 Main Street, Suite B
Tiburon, CA 94920
415-435-9118
415-435-6051 (fax)
hank@hankbrucearchitects.com
www.hankbrucearchitects.com

Fran Halperin & Eric Christ—
Architects
Halperin & Christ
224 Greenfield Avenue, Suite B
San Anselmo, CA 94960
415-457-9185
415-485-6062 (fax)
info@halperinandchrist.com
www.halperinandchrist.com

Hunt Hale Jones Architects
444 Spear Street, Suite 200
San Francisco, CA 94105
415-512-1300
415-288-0288 (fax)
info@hhja.com
www.hunthalejones.com

Patrick Jackson—JDA
Architects & Planners
813 SW Alder Street, Suite 600
Portland, OR 97205
503-228-5426
503-228-5496 (fax)
mail@jda-usa.com

Sandy Walker
Walker & Moody Architects
2666 Hyde Street
San Francisco, CA 94109
415-885-0800
info@walkermoody.com
www.walkermoody.com

Architectural Appliqués

Decorators Supply Corp.
3610 South Morgan Street
Chicago, IL 60609
773-847-6300
773-847-6357 (fax)
www.decoratorssupply.com

Enkeboll Designs
Factory & Showroom
16506 Avalon Boulevard
Carson, CA 90746-1096
800-745-5507
310-532-1400
310-532-2042 (fax)
sales@enkeboll.com
www.enkeboll.com

Renaissance Old World Inc.
1911 S. Parallel Avenue
Fresno, CA 93702
559-444-0558
888-Renaissance
559-445-2635 (fax)
info@carving.com
www.carving.com

Architectural Elements

A L' Ancienne Imports
21800 Schellville Road, Suite D
Sonoma, CA 95476
707-996-2550
707-996-2378 (fax)
info@alaimports.com
www.alancienneimports.com

Ancients, Inc.
9700 Carmel Valley Road
Carmel, CA 93923
831-626-2656
info@AncientsCarmel.com
www.AncientsCarmel.com

Artefact Design & Salvage
23562 Hwy 121
Sonoma, CA 95476
707-933-0660
707-933-0630 (fax)
dave@artefactdesignsalvage.com
www.artefactdesignsalvage.com

Chelsea Antiques
148 Petaluma Boulevard North
Petaluma, CA 94952
707-763-7686
chelseaantiques@earthlink.net

Chelsea Market
132 Petaluma Boulevard North
Petaluma, CA 94952
707-763-2366

Grass Hopper
417 San Anselmo Avenue
San Anselmo, CA 94960
415-455-8580

Jan de Luz
4 East Carmel Valley Road
Carmel, CA 93924
831-659-7966
831-659-7970 (fax)
shops@jandeluz.com
www.jandeluz.com

Off The Wall Architectural
Antiques
On Lincoln between 5th and 6th
Carmel, CA 93921
831-624-6165

Ohmega Salvage
2407 & 2400 San Pablo Avenue
Berkeley, CA 94702-2010
510-204-0767
510-843-7123 (fax)
ohmegasalvage@earthlink.net
www.ohmegasalvage.com

Scott Colombo Designs
341 San Anselmo Avenue
San Anselmo, CA 94960
415-453-5182
www.scottcolombodesigns.com

Sienna
119 Petaluma Boulevard North
Petaluma, CA 94952
707-763-6088

Urban Ore
900 Murray Street
Berkeley, CA 94710-2815
510-841-7283

Architectural Metals

Iron Horse Iron Works
6871 Abbott Avenue
Sebastopol, CA 95472
707-829-0502
707-829-6603 (fax)
ironhorse@sonic.net
www.ironhorseironworks.com

Brian Kennedy
12345 Seigler Canyon Road
Middletown, CA 94561
707-695-6544
brian@thefreedomofcraft.com
www.thefreedomofcraft.com

King Architectural Metals, Inc.
9611 East RL Thornton
  Freeway
Dallas, TX 75228-5618
800-542-2379
214-388-9834
214-388-1048 (fax)
vendorinquiry@kingmetals.com
www.kingmetals.com

Moon Valley Metal
21707 Bonness Road
Sonoma, CA 95476
707-996-1749
bgmsonoma@yahoo.com

Outwater LLC
Architectural Products
East Coast
24 River Road
Bogota, NJ 07603
888-Outwater (688-9283)
800-888-3315 (fax)
West Coast
4720 West Van Buren
P.O. Box 18190
Phoenix, AZ 85043
800-248-2067
www.2.archpro.com

Clyde Wiggins
Lux Metals, Inc.
90 Ridgeway Avenue
Santa Rosa, CA 95404
707-546-1821
707-546-0501 (fax)
caw@sonic.net
luxmetals@sonic.net

Building Materials—New

Golden State Lumber
1100 Anderson Drive
San Rafael, CA 94901
415-454-2532
415-454-6318 (fax)
www.goldenstatelumber.com

Kelleher Corporation
1543 Fifth Avenue
San Rafael, CA 94901
415-454-8861
415-453-1003 (fax)
www.kelleher.com

Home Depot
111 Shoreline Parkway
San Rafael, CA 94901
415-458-8675
www.homedepot.com

Rafael Lumber & Building
  Supply
930 Andersen Drive
San Rafael, CA 94901
415-453-3043
415-453-7031 (fax)
www.rafael-lumber.com

Building Materials —Recycled

Building REsources
701 Amador Street
San Francisco, CA 94124-1234
415-285-7814
415-285-4689 (fax)
brsfcr@yahoo.com
www.buildingresources.org

Rustic Woods Lumber
  Company
4170 Santa Rosa Avenue
Santa Rosa, CA 95407-8267
707-584-7741
rusticwoods@callatg.com

Cabinets

Aurora Cabinets &
  Countertops, Inc.
30 Mark Drive
San Rafael, CA 94903-2260
415-472-4171
415-472-2534 (fax)
info@auroracabinets.com
www.auroracabinets.com

City Cabinetmakers
1351 Underwood Avenue
San Francisco, CA 94124
415-822-6161
415-822-7342 (fax)
v.lopez@citycabinetmakers.com
www.citycabinetmakers.com

Classic Mill & Cabinet
3033 Coffey Lane
Santa Rosa, CA 95403-2582
707-544-7840
707-544-3120 (fax)
www.classicmill.com

Croworks
44 Mariposa Avenue
San Anselmo, CA 94960
415-454-6809
vwcroworks@yahoo.com

Gary Arrigo
Design-Line Cabinetry
58 Paul Drive, Suite 12
San Rafael, CA 94903
415-456-4166
415-459-2470 (fax)

Gordon Abbott Cabinetmaker
55 Manzanita Avenue
Black Point, CA 94945
415-328-6052

John Hull
Linda Applewhite & Associates
510 Turney Street
Sausalito, CA 94965
415-331-2040
415-331-2070 (fax)
info@lindaapplewhite.com
www.lindaapplewhite.com

J. Russel Tunder Cabinet-
  Design
68 Woodland Avenue, Suite E
San Rafael, CA 94901
415-454-4453
rtunder@yahoo.com

Sierra Woodworks
3236 Fitzgerald Road, Suite H
Rancho Cordova, CA 95742-
  6814
916-635-2680
916-635-9543 (fax)

Sonoma Valley Woodworks
1770 Napa Road
Sonoma, CA 95476
707-939-9307

Sweetheart Cabinetmakers
360 Sutton Place
Santa Rosa, CA 95407-8121
707-588-0171
800-994-9279
707-588-0175 (fax)
info@sweetheartcabinets.com
www.sweetheartcabinets.com

Cabinet Doors

Decore-ative Specialties
2772 South Peck Road
Monrovia, CA 91016
877-4-DECORE
info@decore.com
www.decore.com

Cabinet Legs

Classic Designs
84 Central Street
St. Johnsbury, VT 05819
800-843-7405
802-748-4350 (fax)
legs@tablelegs.com
www.tablelegs.com

Concrete

Bay Area Concretes Inc
4179 Business Center Drive
Fremont, CA 94538-6355
510-651-6020
www.bayareaconcretes.com

Buddy Rhodes Studio
691 Tennessee Street
San Francisco, CA 94107
877-706-5303
415-431-8070
415-551-1575 (fax)
info@buddyrhodes.com
www.buddyrhodes.com

Napa Valley Cast Stone
1111 Green Island Road
American Canyon, CA 94558
707-258-3340
707-258-3350 (fax)
sales@napavalleycaststone.com
www.napavalleycaststone.com

Sonoma Cast Stone
133 Copeland Street
Petaluma, CA 94952
877-283-2400
707-283-1888
707-283-1899 (fax)
sales@sonomastone.com
www.sonomastone.com

Contractors

Frey Plastering, Inc.
898 Vallejo Avenue
Novato, CA 94945
415-897-4510

Ireland-Robinson & Hadley Inc.
85 Beach Road
Belvedere, CA 94920
415-383-0583

Charles D. Kuhn Inc.
P.O. Box 151676
San Rafael, CA 94915
415-883-7506
415-382-1216 (fax)

James G. Lino Construction
P.O. Box 719
Point Reyes Station, CA 94956
415-663-1939

Terry Rochester
Roc Builders
600 Spring Street
Sausalito, CA 94965
415-332-8433

Duncan Wilson Construction
818 Rincon Way
San Rafael, CA 94903
415-479-6269
415-479-6258 (fax)
duncanwilsonconst@comcast.net
www.duncanwilsonconstruc-
 tion.com

Doors and Windows

Andersen Corporation
100 Fourth Avenue North
Bayport, MN 55003-1096
888-888-7020
www.andersenwindows.com

Blomberg Building Materials Inc.
Headquarters Location
1453 Blair Avenue
Sacramento, CA 95822
 916-428-8060
916-422-1967 (fax)

Jeld-Wen, Inc. (Formerly Pozzi
 Windows & Doors)
P.O. Box 1329
Klamath Falls, OR 97601
800-535-3936
www.jeld-wen.com

Marvin Windows and Doors
P.O. Box 100
Warroad, MN 56763
888-537-7828
www.marvin.com

Mission Wood Products Inc.
27 Paul Drive
San Rafael, CA 94903
415-472-2280

Ocean Sash and Door Inc.
3154 17th Street
San Francisco, CA 94110
415-863-1256
415-863-6218 (fax)
www.oceansashanddoor

Simpson Door Company
400 Simpson Avenue
McCleary, WA 98557
1-800-952-4057
simpsondoor@brandner.com
www.simpsondoor.com

Sonoma Door & Sash
19500 8th Street East
Sonoma, CA 95476-3801
707-938-3719

Southwest Door & Window of
 CA, Inc.
322 E. Cota Street
Santa Barbara, CA 93101
805-966-4263
 805-568-0774 (fax)
info@swdoor.com
www.swdoor.com

Window Warehouse
5776 Paradise Drive
Corte Madera, CA 94925
415-924-8300
415-924-4509 (fax)
www.windowwarehouse.net

Faux Finish Artisans

Arno Cornillon
10 Friendship Street
Tivoli, NY 12583
845-757-5090

Shawn Man Roland
Linda Applewhite & Associates
510 Turney Street
Sausalito, CA 94965
415-331-2040
415-331-2070 (fax)
info@lindaapplewhite.com
www.lindaapplewhite.com

Fireplaces

Blaze Fireplaces
101 Cargo Way
San Francisco, CA 94124
415-495-2002
415-495-2446 (fax)
www.blazefireplaces.com

Buckley Rumford Company
1035 Monroe Street
Port Townsend, WA 98368
360-385-9974
360-385-9483
360-385-1624 (fax)
buckley@rumford.com
www.rumford.com

London Chimney
267 Shoreline Highway
Mill Valley, CA 94941
415-383-8227 Marin
415-931-3838 SF
service@londonchimney.com
www.londonchim.com

Okell's Fireplace
1300 17th Street
San Francisco, CA 94107
415-626-1110
www.okellsfireplace.com

Fireplace Boxes

Heat & Glo
A Brand of Hearth & Home
 Technologies Inc.
Corporate Office
20802 Kensington Boulevard
Lakeville, MN 55044
888-427-3973
info@heatnglo.com
www.heatnglo.com

Lennox Hearth Products
1110 West Taft Avenue
Orange, CA 92865-4150
info@lennox.com
www.lennoxhearthproducts.com

Martin Hearth and Heating
149 Cleveland Drive
Paris, KY 40361
www.martinindustries.com

Fireplace Screens
Brian Kennedy
12345 Seigler Canyon Road
Middletown, CA 94561
707-695-6544
brian@thefreedomofcraft.com
www.thefreedomofcraft.com

Iron Horse Iron Works
6871 Abbott Avenue
Sebastopol, CA 95472
707-829-0502
707-829-6603 (fax)
ironhorse@sonic.net
www.ironhorseironworks.com

Moon Valley Metal
21707 Bonness Road
Sonoma, CA 95476
707-996-1749
bgmsonoma@yahoo.com

Flooring
First, Last & Always
Custom Floors
P.O. Box 31776
San Francisco, CA 94131
415-753-8627
415-546-0451 (fax)
info@first-last-always.com
www.first-last-always.com

Handloggers Flooring, LLC
305 Cutting Boulevard
Pt. Richmond, CA 94804
510-231-6190
510-231-6199 (fax)
tim@handloggers.com
www.handloggersflooring.com

Hardware
Baldwin Brass Center
2119 San Pablo Avenue
Berkeley, CA 94702-1827
510-548-5757
510-548-4342 (fax)
www.belmonthardware.com

Bauerware
3886 17th Street
San Francisco, CA 94114
415-864-3886
415-864-3889 (fax)
inquiries@bauerware.com
www.bauerware.com

Bouvet USA
1060 Illinois Street
San Francisco, CA 94109
415-864-0273
415-864-2068 (fax)
Request@bouvet.com
www.bouvet.com

Emtek
800-356-2741
800-577-5771 (fax)
www.emtekproducts.com

Gerber Hinge Company
21034 Osborne Street
Canoga Park, CA 91304-1744
800-643-7237
818-717-5016 (fax)
info@gerberhinge.com
www.gerber-hinge.com

Arnaud Massonnat
The Golden Lion *Office*
3815 Grand View Boulevard
Los Angeles, CA 90066
877-398-2848
310-398-0605 (fax)
Showroom
225 N. Robertson Boulevard
Beverly Hills, CA 90211
310-246-1752
310-246-1691
arnaud@thegoldenlion.com
www.thegoldenlion.com

Forged Iron Hardware by Acorn
Garbe Industries, Inc.
4137 S. 72nd East Avenue
Tulsa, Oklahoma 74145
800-735-2241
918-627-4598 (fax)
information@garbes.com
www.garbes.com/hardware

Ironware International
2421 Cruzen Street
Nashville, TN 37211
615-726-2500
615-726-2509 (fax)
info@ironwareinternational.com
www.ironwareinternational.com

Jackson's Hardware
435 Du Bois Street
San Rafael, CA 94901-5344
415-454-3740

LB Brass
3100 47th Avenue
Long Island City, NY 11101
718-786-8090
718-786-5060 (fax)
LB@lbbrass.com
www.lbbrass.com

Maguire Iron Corporation
215-22nd Street
Richmond, CA 94801
510-234-7569
510-232-7519 (fax)
www.maguireironcorporation.com

Rocky Mountain Hardware
P.O. Box 4108
1030 Airport Way
Hailey, Idaho 83333
208-788-2013
888-788-2013
208-788-2577 (fax)
info@rockymountainhardware.com
www.rockymountainhardware.com

Lighting
Arte De Mexico
5356 Riverton Avenue
North Hollywood, CA 91601
818-769-5090
818-769-9425 (fax)
sales@artedemexico.com
www.artedemexico.com

Corbett Lighting
14625 East Clark Avenue
City of Industry, CA 91745
626-336-4511
626-330-4266 (fax)
www.corbettlighting.com

City Lights
1585 Folsom Street
San Francisco, CA 94103
415-863-2020
415-621-6050 (fax)
www.citylightssf.com

Hudson Valley Lighting, Inc.
106 Pierces Road
P.O. Box 7459
Newburgh, NY 12550
845-561-0300
845-561-6848 (fax)
www.hudsonvalleylighting.com

The Malder Company
1157 Folsom Street
San Francisco, CA 94103
415-626-9492
415-626-9693 (fax)

Jim Misner Light Designs
2988 Washington Street
San Francisco, CA 94115
415-928-0400 (phone/fax)
info@jimmisnerlightdesigns.com
www.jimmisnerlightdesigns.com

Omega Too
2204 San Pablo Avenue
Berkeley, CA 94702
510-843-3636
510-843-0666 (fax)
megatoo@pacbell.net
www.omegatoo.com

Rejuvenation Inc.
2550 NW Nicolai Street
Portland, OR 97210
888-401-1900
800-526-7329 (fax)
info@rejuvenation.com
www.rejuvenation.com

Revival Lighting
4860 Rainier Avenue South
Seattle, WA 98118
206-722-4404
info@revivallighting.com
www.revivallighting.com

Mantels

Foster Mantels
30489 San Antonio Street
Hayward, CA 94544
800-285-8551
inquiry@mantels.net
www.mantels.net

California Mantel, Inc.
P.O. Box 340037
Sacramento, CA 95834-0037
916-925-5775
916-925-5797 (fax)
sales@calmantel.com
www.calmantel.com

Napa Valley Cast Stone
1111 Green Island Road
American Canyon, CA 94558
707-258-3340
707-258-3350 (fax)
sales@napavalleycaststone.com
www.napavalleycaststone.com

Sonoma Cast Stone
133 Copeland Street
Petaluma, CA 94952
877-283-2400
707-283-1888
707-283-1899 (fax)
sales@sonomastone.com
www.sonomastone.com

Tile & Stone Concepts, Inc.
1505 East Francisco Boulevard
San Rafael, CA 94901
415-457-9422
415-457-2904 (fax)
info@tile-stone.com
www.tile-stone.com

Moldings

Kelleher Corporation
1543 Fifth Avenue
San Rafael, CA 94901
415-454-8861
415-453-1003 (fax)
www.kelleher.com

San Francisco Victoriana, Inc.
2070 Newcomb Avenue
San Francisco, CA 94124
415-648-0313
415-648-2812 (fax)
www.sfvictoriana.com

White River Hardwoods
  Woodworks Inc.
1197 Happy Hollow Road
Fayetteville, AR 72701
800-558-0119
www.mouldings.com

Paints

Benjamin Moore & Company
51 Chestnut Ridge Road
Montvale, NJ 07645
800-344-0400
info@benjaminmoore.com
www.benjaminmoore.com

Dunn Edwards
888-DE PAINT
www.dunnedwards.com

Martin Senour
www.martinsenour.com

Pratt Lambert
800-289-7728
www.prattandlambert.com

Sydney Harbour Paint Company
801 Mateo Street
Los Angeles, CA 90021
877-228-8440
213-228-8977 (fax)
shpco@sbcglobal.net
www.sydneyharbourpaints.com

Tamalpais Paint & Color
30 Tamalpais Drive
Corte Madera, CA 94925
415-924-7321

Skylights

Window Warehouse
5776 Paradise Drive
Corte Madera, CA 94925
415-924-8300
415-924-4509 (fax)
www.windowwarehouse.net

Stucco

LaHabra
P.O. Box 17866
4125 East LaPalma, Suite 250
Anaheim, CA 92807
714-778-2266
714-774-2079 (fax)
Toll Free: 877-LHSTUCCO
info@lahabrastucco.com
www.lahabrastucco.com

Tile and Stone

Napa Valley Cast Stone
1111 Green Island Road
American Canyon, CA 94558
707-258-3340
707-258-3350 (fax)
sales@napavalleycaststone.com
www.napavalleycaststone.com

Sonoma Cast Stone
133 Copeland Street
Petaluma, CA 94952
877-283-2400
707-283-1888
707-283-1899 (fax)
sales@sonomastone.com
www.sonomastone.com

Tile & Stone Concepts, Inc.
1505 East Francisco Boulevard
San Rafael, CA 94901
415-457-9422
415-457-2904 (fax)
info@tile-stone.com
www.tile-stone.com

Wallflowering

Zdravko Terziev Designs
415-924-5147
www.wallflowering.com

Window Film

3M Window Film
888-364-3577
www.3m.com